Skills in Relational Coaching

Skills in Relational Coaching

Simon Cavicchia
Charlotte Sills

1 Oliver's Yard
55 City Road
London EC1Y 1SP

2455 Teller Road
Thousand Oaks
California 91320

Unit No 323-333, Third Floor, F-Block
International Trade Tower, Nehru Place
New Delhi 110 019

8 Marina View Suite 43-053
Asia Square Tower 1
Singapore 018960

Editor: Susannah Trefgarne
Editorial assistant: Harry Dixon
Production editor: Rabia Barkatulla
Copyeditor: Diana Chambers
Indexer: Elizabeth Ball
Marketing manager: Ben Sherwood
Cover design: Sheila Tong
Typeset by: KnowledgeWorks Global Ltd.
Printed and bound by CPI Group (UK) Ltd
Croydon, CR0 4YY

Library of Congress Control Number: 2024948438

British Library Cataloguing in Publication data

A catalogue record for this book is available from the British Library

ISBN 9781529793918
ISBN 9781529793901 (pbk)

CONTENTS

ABOUT THE AUTHORS

Simon Cavicchia is an executive coach, team coach and coach supervisor. He consults leaders, teams and organisations facing complex challenges, where human connection and developing the capacity to think together is central to navigating these situations creatively. He has a background in Gestalt psychotherapy, psychoanalytic and systems thinking. He was Joint Programme Director of the Masters in Coaching Psychology at the Metanoia Institute in London. He is currently a member of faculty on the Ashridge-Hult Masters in Executive Coaching in the UK. For the last 30 years Simon has been interested in relational ideas and how they might inform coaching, leadership and organisation development. He has written on the theory and practice of relational coaching, relational team coaching and the experience of shame in organisational life and its role in driving disconnection and undermining creativity and collaboration.

He continues to explore ways of normalising ordinary human vulnerabilities so that they can be understood and thought about in ways that support greater depth of connection between individuals and the organisations they participate in creating. On working with Charlotte, Simon says: 'Collaborating with Charlotte on this book has been a joy. Charlotte's kindness, warmth, clarity of thinking and playful intelligence have brought richness and depth to our conversations as well as lightness and fun in times of stuckness. I am proud of what we have written and grateful for our friendship that has deepened as a result of our work together'.

Charlotte Sills is an experienced coach and coach supervisor and Professor of Coaching at Hult Ashridge Business School where she is a member of faculty on the Ashridge Masters in Executive Coaching programmes and the postgraduate Diploma in Organisational Supervision, both of which offer a relational approach. Before joining Ashridge, Charlotte was a member of the leadership team and Head of the Transactional Analysis Department at Metanoia Institute, London and worked in private practice as a psychotherapist, coach and trainer/consultant in a variety of organisations, particularly in the area of mental health. She has taught all over the world and published widely in the fields of therapy and coaching, including co-authoring several books on Relational Transactional Analysis and Gestalt.

On working with Simon, Charlotte says; 'This has been a wonderful journey – stimulating, interesting – and often hilarious. Simon is a lovely and generous man and also the most erudite, eloquent and witty person you could ever hope to meet. It has been wonderful to be working with him and I am delighted that we are continuing to develop the Cavicchia-Sills offering'.

PREFACE

WHY FOCUS ON THE RELATIONSHIP?

In writing this book, we have drawn upon our experience of many years exploring and applying relational ideas in coaching, psychotherapy, teaching and organisational consulting. Simply put, relational practice sees relationship as central to how we develop as human beings, make sense of the world and organise our behaviour in service of community and our wider humanity. In Chapter 1 we briefly set out the principles informing a relational approach to coaching. The rest of the book describes the skills and practices that support this way of working.

We believe that these ideas and the practical skills that emerge from them are more important now than ever for coaches and anyone concerned with contributing to re-balancing the emphasis placed on individualism in organisations and wider society. We see increasing evidence that, as a species, we are retreating into a particular form of hyper-individualism that drives isolation, disconnection and self-serving protectionism. It was not always this way. In the nineteenth century, individualism was a philosophical and ethical perspective that allowed each person to respect the dignity of, and cooperate with, others – all sharing equal rights for the beneficial evolution of community as a whole. The Italian political theorist Nadia Urbinati (2015) describes how today, individualism has given rise to 'individualists' who are more self-interested and whose maxim might be best expressed as 'I don't give a damn'. This contemporary form of individualism is fuelled by mounting anxiety in the face of socioeconomic and geopolitical instability, along with increasing evidence of the climate emergency that is progressing at an alarming rate. It is characterised by possessiveness, conformity and litigiousness, and for many who are disillusioned, is passive in relation to participation in social and community life.

These extremes of contemporary hyper-individualism lie at the heart of ideologies such as far-right populism with its emphasis on protecting the interests of whichever defined and separate group is deemed to be superior. This inevitably leads to the exclusion, othering and demonisation of those who do not share in the characteristics valued by the chosen. It can be seen in economic neoliberalism which has long celebrated and venerated competition between individuals, considering it to be the driving force for economic growth, colluding in a fantasy (given current factual realities such as gross global wealth inequalities) that this has 'trickle down' benefits for all.

This disturbing trend inevitably gives rise to processes of relating that perpetuate and exacerbate the self-serving competitive manipulation of other human beings. It is borne of and perpetuates masculine ideals such as the lonely hero archetype in organisations and the 'strong man' in political life, where individual strength and power are celebrated and any ordinary vulnerability or need for human connection is equated with weakness or effeminacy. It finds its way into identity politics, celebrating difference and disappearing the need also for shared interests and projects calling for collaboration and connection. Here individual groups of the disenfranchised end up attacking and competing with other groups of the disenfranchised in order to progress their individual agendas. While it is often well intentioned and vital to value and appreciate differences, especially where these differentiating features have been marginalised within prevailing norms and ideologies, this can also fuel rigidification of individual identity groups to the exclusion of others. The forces of hyper-individualism can be at work even in those projects that claim to be working for a greater collective good, especially those that insist on silencing any voices deemed to be dissenting, eroding free speech upon which democracy depends.

Hyper-individualism, in all its forms, is ultimately a lonely and isolating pursuit. While as human beings we all need times to be separate and feel the uniqueness of our experience, we also need to be able to connect, for our mental health and well-being, with a world and other individuals outside of ourselves. Hyper-individualism as an invisible force privileges the former and disappears the latter. This drives cycles of seeking to fill the emptiness that this gives rise to in the form of addictions, wealth, status, lifestyle, the control and manipulation of others who are no longer seen as subjects, but as objects to be exploited for our individual needs and concerns – and the list goes on.

There is much to be undone.

Our work over many years as psychotherapists and relational coaches has allowed us to see first-hand the pain caused by the pressures of living up to the demands of hyper-individualism. It has also allowed us to experience the power of re-establishing connection to oneself and to others in freeing people from the 'tyranny of the moderns' as Nadia Urbinati (2015) calls it in the title of her book.

This work is hard but worthwhile. In our own small way, we hope this book might help to restore the balance, raising awareness of unhelpful patterns of relating and igniting curiosity about and enjoyment of real connection between human beings and the development of vibrant generative contact. We make no grandiose promises as this would be leaning into another consequence of contemporary individualism – the pursuit of quick fixes in service of control. Instead, we offer perspectives and practices that coaches and psychotherapists wanting to integrate more relational perspectives into their lives and practice might make use of in this project.

This book would not have been possible without relationships. We are grateful for all of those who in a multitude of ways have contributed to the ideas and chapters that follow.

We count ourselves blessed to be participating and held in networks and communities of relationships, our partners, families, friends, colleagues and the many students who we have had the privilege of teaching and continue to connect with as part of alumni networks.

We would like to specifically mention our partners Fabrice Lamotte and Phil Joyce, and our colleagues on the faculty at Ashridge – Ann Knights, David Birch, Dorothee Stoffels, Erik de Haan, Judith Bell and Tammy Tawadros who exemplify a commitment to relationship, support, dialogue and being a true 'community' of practice. Our clients over the years have taught us much through their own willingness to enter into the good-natured struggle of restoring connection to themselves and others in the world, at times influencing the quality of relationship in their own networks and organisations, as have our students who have enabled us to explore, think and refine the ideas that follow, and who continue to creatively contribute to furthering relational practice and the thawing of hyper-individualism one relationship at a time.

We are enormously appreciative of Susannah Trefgarne and Harry Dixon at SAGE for their patience, warmth, encouragement and guidance. And a huge thank you to editor and 'lay reader' extraordinaire Lil Chase, whose energy and enthusiasm and brilliant skills galvanised us immeasurably.

Finally, we want to celebrate each other and our relationship. It has been deeply rewarding, and *fun* to create something together.

1
WHAT IS RELATIONAL COACHING?

> Relationship is the first condition of being human … It is so obvious that it is frequently taken for granted, and so mysterious that many of the world's greatest psychologists, novelists and philosophers have made it a focal point of a lifetime's preoccupying passion.
>
> (Petrūska Clarkson, 1995, p. 4)

THE RELATIONAL TURN

Human beings are conceived in relationship. We develop and are shaped in relationship. It is in relationship that we grow and change.

Developmental psychology and affective neuroscience research have amply demonstrated the central role of relationships and the quality of interaction in our early development as human beings (Stern, 1985; Siegel, 1999; Schore, 2003, 2009). These experiences are fundamental to shaping our personalities, our beliefs and our assumptions about the world. As adults, they form our capacity for reflecting on and creatively navigating the challenges of being human.

Attachment theory (Bowlby, 1969, 1973) and the neuroscience research of the Boston Change Process Study Group (2010) show that we remain sensitive to the quality of our connections with others throughout our lives; they help us feel safe and manage anxiety and stress (Porges, 2011). Relationships – our ability to form and maintain them, find new supportive connections when they come along and mourn them when they come to an end – are therefore fundamental to our mental health. Our capacity to think, come together, organise and co-ordinate to respond to complex organisational and global challenges (like the Covid pandemic and climate emergency) are all dependent, therefore, upon relationships.

What Do We Mean by Relational Coaching?

The 'relational turn', be it in coaching, consulting, psychotherapy, developmental neuroscience, art, philosophy or sociology, represents quite possibly the most significant shift in perspective of the twentieth and twenty-first centuries. At its heart, it's an awakening to the centrality of interconnectedness and relationship that pervades all human development and processes in the natural world. This focus on relationship and dynamic interactions between people and nature also extends to the sociological and political realms of culture, ideology, meaning-making and the evolution of ideas – therefore, humanity itself. It even extends to the scientific domain with developments in quantum physics pointing to the dynamic process and interactions of subatomic particles.

This way of 'relational' thinking stands in marked contrast to established ways of perceiving the world that have dominated human consciousness in the Western world for centuries and, in some areas, still persists today. Prior to the relational turn, which has its roots in the late nineteenth- and early twentieth-century humanistic movement (Buber, 1965; Kant, 1965; Nietzsche, 1966; Merleau Ponty, 1969; Levinas, 1989), the emphasis was on linear cause-and-effect assumptions embedded in Newtonian physics. The isolated individual was sovereign and relationships were only relevant in terms of how they could be exploited to enable the *individual* to achieve his or her needs and goals (Carrol and Shaw, 2013). This individualistic bias extended to the ways in which organisations have been constructed and studied. It has also influenced organisations globally so that even in, for example, South Asian and Asian companies where a more collective culture might be expected, individualism too often reigns.

The individualistic view emphasised competitive striving and certainly resulted in many achievements. However, the over-privileging of the individual or 'isolated' organisation has also resulted in a failure to appreciate the inevitable interconnectedness of human life where the actions (and inactions) of individuals cannot but have wide-reaching consequences on other individuals. In the climate crisis, we have a very real example of how the chickens of individualism and a blindness to unfettered extraction of global resources have come home to roost. It is also worrying that this reality, while acting as a spur to collective action in some areas, is also leading some individuals and groups to rigidify their individual and national interests in the face of this existential threat to our collective survival. For us, this makes the case for a relational orientation to coaching even stronger. The leaders, organisations and systems of human endeavour that are leaning into the interconnectedness of all human life are awakening to the wide-reaching impacts of their actions and their moral, ethical and existential obligations.

What Do We Mean by a Relational Coach?

A relational coach is one who believes that the process of human relating is the most important factor in creating what is happening in the world at every level – it shapes the development of individuals and communities, including organisations – and it is also the main vehicle for change. Therefore, the relational coach is continuously interested in the way a client relates to themself, their colleagues, their family, friends, work colleagues, the communities they are part of – and, of course their client. This means that the coach's work will tend to be largely 'present-centred'. In other words, they will be looking to work with relational patterns both inside and outside the coaching room and relationship.

This book is concerned with what this 'working with' involves and the orientations and skills in the coach that support this practice.

Why is there such a Focus on Processes of Relating?

One of the most compelling reasons for taking a relational approach to coaching is the now established body of research spanning over 70 years that demonstrates the central role of the relationship between practitioner and client in determining effective outcomes of psychotherapy (Horvath and Symonds, 1991; Martin et al., 2000; Wampold, 2001, cited in De Haan and Sills, 2012). While this research has taken place mainly in the field of psychotherapy, de Haan and Sills (2012) state that the field of psychotherapy and coaching 'have enough in common – in the sense that they both involve intentional use of a relationship to further the development of a client – to make these conclusions highly relevant for practitioners in both fields' (p. 4). Also, subsequent research into coaching outcome supports similar findings, although different studies highlight other 'active ingredients' also (see, e.g., De Haan 2021; De Haan et al., 2016) such as resilience in the client and the clarity of the contract.

Meta-analysis research (see, e.g., Asay and Lambert, 1999; Wampold, 2001; Norcross and Lambert, 2019) has identified a number of these active ingredients that make for effective outcomes. Among these is a series of 'common factors' that are common across all the multitude of approaches therapists and, by extension, coaches, might use.

These common factors have to do with:

- The setting for the work, including meeting at regular intervals, offering a belief and expectation that change and development can happen.
- The client's level of commitment and desire to be helped, including their expectations, preferences and support networks.

In addition to the factors above, there are three common factors that are particularly relevant for a relational orientation to coaching:

- The quality of presence, warmth, depth, listening, empathy that the coach brings to the relationship along with a capacity to put to one side their own values system and world views in order to communicate with the client's values system.
- The dynamics of the interactive relational field that coach and client co-create together – i.e., what happens between them, the quality of communication, trust and agreement about the nature of the shared coaching endeavour.
- There is also evidence to suggest that the practitioner's level of commitment to and belief in his work and approach is significant.

De Haan and Sills (2012) summarise the implications of this research for coaching practice and those factors that contribute to successful coaching as:

- A relationship, as experienced by the client, of respect and empathy combined with a shared agreement about goals and the nature of the work.
- An authentic meeting where the coach shows a clear allegiance to an approach but holds it lightly while responding to the preferences and frames of reference of the client.
- Client factors, including motivation and 'hope' as well a supportive family, friends and the organisational context.
- Practitioner qualities such as attractiveness, flexibility and warmth.
- An opportunity for the client to explore himself and his thoughts and feelings as well as try out new behaviour.
- Seeking feedback from the client about what they experience as helpful.
- No attempt to match – for example, the coach's gender, race or religion with the client's (unless the client strongly requests this) – but an offer of curiosity and interest into the client's culture and views.

In addition to the research we have summarised above, we also want to acknowledge a powerful confluence of many aspects of human understanding in recent years under the overarching concept of the 'relational turn'. We want to set out those areas that have particular relevance for coaching as these represent aspects of the wider context in which coaching as a profession and practice is situated, as well as dynamics and issues for which a relational approach to coaching is particularly well suited.

Relational Perspectives on Organisations and Organisational Learning

Another consequence of the relational turn is that the prevailing view of organisations has been evolving – from a view of an organisation as a well-oiled (or badly oiled) machine (very much a construct of the mechanistic individualist era), to seeing organisations as connected to, influencing and influenced by their relationship to the environment, as in the open systems approach to organisational research (Hirschhorn and Barnett, 1993). More recently still, a view has emerged from chaos and complexity theory that sees organisations as communities of interactive practices (Stacey, 2001, 2003) or 'contexts of human endeavour' (Cavicchia and Gilbert, 2018). Here, organisations are conceived of as being primarily processes of relating and 'conversing' between members of that organisation. Hence, they are seen as dynamic entities with permeable boundaries.

Perspectives on leadership have also evolved from the hierarchical, lonely hero archetype of early formulations of what it means to lead, to seeing leaders as embedded in networks and wider ecological systems. In order for a leader to achieve their objectives, they need to connect others and connect with others (Western, 2013; Critchley, 2021). The role of leadership is also seen to be expanding beyond the primary objectives of increasing profit and shareholder value, to the notion of leaders and their organisations being stewards for the well-being of members of the organisation and guardians of the impacts on the wider global ecosystem (Eisenstein 2011, 2013; Western, 2013). These developments are in part a response to the increasing volatility, uncertainty, complexity and ambiguity (VUCA) that are seen to characterise contemporary organisational life, as well as shifting perceptions and expectations among the customers and stakeholders that organisations serve. It is no longer possible for leaders to respond to novel and unpredictable changes by doing more of the same and expecting a different result. For Einstein, this approach was the definition of madness.

Researchers into the evolution of human consciousness (Cook-Greuter, 2004; Torbert, 2004; O'Fallon, 2012; Laloux, 2014) have described developmental shifts that occur in individuals as they open up to more expanded perspectives on leadership than simply the active, achievement-and-goal oriented constructs that have dominated human consciousness for centuries. Goals remain important but, as individuals develop their perspective, there is an opening to a greater appreciation of how different individuals make sense of and construct reality. This appreciation brings with it the possibility for leaders to work more with individuals and in relationship to unlock collective wisdom and innovation that goes untapped, or even actively suppressed, in more hierarchical, command-and-control approaches to leadership. This mirrors calls from a number of leadership researchers who have been describing the need for leaders to bring to work more of themselves and who they are as people (Hirschhorn, 1998). Today's organisational challenges cannot be resolved with one senior leader having all the answers. Instead, individuals, irrespective of rank, need to be able to come together, relate, speak freely, befriend inevitable uncertainty and not knowing in order to unlock the collective power to strategise for organisational success, adaptability and survival.

From this we draw a number of principles that for us underpin a relational orientation to coaching.

RELATIONAL PRINCIPLES

1 The quality of the relationship between coach and client and the dynamics between them are key to creating conditions supportive of development and growth.
2 Human beings develop in and are shaped by relationships throughout their lives. They mutually influence one another consciously and unconsciously in relationship and this can be made use of for supporting learning and change.
3 We make meaning and sense of our experience in relationship.
4 Meaning about ourselves, others and the world is 'socially constructed'. In relationships, there is no single truth.
5 Whenever people come together, there are two levels of relating happening: the 'explicit' – the content of our conversation, thoughts, overt communication. The 'implicit' – the feeling of being together which is felt but not yet articulated.
6 Patterns of thinking (assumptions, beliefs), feelings and behaviour are developed in early relationships and re-enacted in the present moment with the coach and others in the client's networks. The same is true of the coach's patterns of relating.
7 Our sense of self as a coherent experience of 'going on' and having resources to draw upon is inextricably bound up with the nature and quality of our connection to others and the environment.
8 A relational orientation to coaching pays close attention to the wider context in which coaching takes place and has an ethical stance which is concerned with minimising harm to individuals, communities and the wider ecology which sustains all relationships and human life itself.

OUTLINE OF THE BOOK

Each chapter draws upon the principles above and considers implications for relational coaching practice and the skills and orientations required of the coach.

In Chapter 2 we pay attention to how the coach can work with the client to co-create and maintain the conditions and qualities of relationship supportive of learning and development and we explore contracting from a relational perspective, Principle 1.

In Chapter 3 we describe relational coaching as a process of collaborative enquiry where the subjective realities of coach and client, including similarities and differences, meet in the coaching relationship and provide a rich source of experience to draw upon for thinking together, making meaning, expanding perspectives and generating options for action. Principles 2, 3, 4.

In Chapter 4, we focus on the coach, their experience moment by moment and their 'use of self' being core elements in enabling learning and growth with the client. We offer a model describing how coaches can make use of their felt experience to reflect and shape their interventions with coaches. Principles 3, 4, 5.

In Chapter 5, we explore the way in which past experiences of relationship have shaped our beliefs, assumptions and ways of being in the world and how these can reveal themselves and be responded to in the present moment of working with a client. Principle 6.

In Chapter 6, we explore how the quality of the coaching relationship and the dynamics between coach and client can sometimes result in each unhelpfully re-enacting stuck patterns from their past. We offer ways of learning from and working with these patterns as they arise. Principles 6 and 7.

In Chapter 7, we focus on skills and strategies for experimenting with clients to bring about increased awareness and new possibilities for action where these might be required. We stress the importance, in a relational orientation to coaching, of any experiment needing to be informed by the coach's experience of being with the client moment by moment. Principles 6 and 7.

In Chapter 8, we explore transitions and endings in coaching and organisational life and how the coach might work with these. Principle 8.

We end the book in Chapter 9 by considering the ethical and moral dimensions of relational coaching. We compare a relational orientation with the more individualistic assumptions that drive behaviour in society, cultures and organisational life, and describe the crucial importance of fostering relationship in service of facing threats to our well-being and survival as a species. Principle 9.

CONCLUSION

In this chapter we have attempted to describe briefly the ideas and principles behind the relational approach to coaching. We present it as the intentional use of relationship – prioritising the processes of relating – supported by the recognition of the importance of relationship in all human endeavour.

For the rest of the book, we focus on relational practice and the orientations, skills and attitudes that coaches wishing to work relationally will need to cultivate.

2

ESTABLISHING THE WORKING ALLIANCE: CONTACTING AND CONTRACTING

> There are three elements of 'the working alliance' – 'goals', 'tasks' and 'bonds'.
>
> (Bordin, 1979, 1994)

The coaching pair form an agreement about what the coaching is intended to achieve (goals), as well as an understanding of how they will work together (tasks) – what they can expect from themselves and each other. The final element – the bonds – means that they will establish and seek to maintain a relationship of mutual trust and respect that can survive any difficulties along the way. These apparently straightforward aspects of relating are easier said than done.

In this chapter, we explore these three elements. They are at the heart of the relationship that is the essential core of effective psychotherapy and coaching (Luborsky et al., 1975; Horvath and Symonds, 1991; Orlinsky et al., 1994; Asay and Lambert, 1999; Martin et al., 2000; De Haan et al., 2016; Flückiger et al., 2017; Horvath, 2018). Despite the abundance of different definitions and descriptions of contracting (see, e.g., Horvath and Greenberg, 1994) and, in particular, those authors who have attempted to emphasise the relational elements of human encounter (see, e.g., Safran and Muran, 2006), we make use of the model developed by one of the earliest writers on the subject – Edward Bordin (1979, 1994). We will use his framework for examining the key elements that establish a relationship between coach and client that allow them to work collaboratively and creatively together. This model honours the needs of the individual as they enter relationship.

We explore all three here in reverse order, starting with 'Bonds'.

BONDS

Mutual trust is a quality of relationship that allows the client to feel accepted and not judged, even when they have begun to reveal (to themselves as well as to the coach) those parts of themselves that they are most anxious about, unsure of, or ashamed of. The process of building this empathic bond starts at the first moment of contact. Recent developments in neurobiology let us know that the mind is in a constant state of assessing and forming hypotheses about the environment. Porges's (2009) concept of neuroception states that human beings are constantly scanning others for cues of safety and danger. These cues can be anything from their similarity to someone in our past, through to the tension in their facial muscles or the size of their pupils. Human beings are very adept at reading signals. The coach aims to genuinely offer what is needed to allow the client to feel 'safe enough'. A feeling of total safety would mean that not much change would happen as there would be little or no challenge. Whereas *too much* challenge and feeling unsafe would feel too threatening and prevent the client opening up to learning.

This empathic bond is best characterised by Rogers's (1951) six conditions for change:

1 The coaching pair is in contact.
2 The client is willing to be known by the other.
3 The coach offers the so called 'core condition' of empathy.
4 The coach offers the 'core condition' of respect.
5 The coach offers the 'core condition' of authenticity.
6 Crucially, the client receives these three core conditions.

But how can the coach embody the core conditions?

The answer is to do our own inner work. Our colleagues, Robin Shohet and Joan Wilmot, ask the question: 'What is getting in the way of my loving this client?' They believe that the natural state of human connection is love and that fear is the only obstacle to love. This fear arises from our own past patterns – our 'script' (Berne, 1961), our resentments or perceived inadequacies, our envy or competitiveness. If we do our own work – either through self-reflection or with a therapist or coach – we can learn to love and accept ourselves and therefore we will find ourselves able to offer empathy, respect and authenticity to our clients.

SKILLS FOR OFFERING EMPATHY, RESPECT AND AUTHENTICITY

Empathy

The coach expresses empathy when they communicate understanding of what the client is experiencing and the client experiences being understood. This understanding is conveyed through facial expression, voice tone, right-brain to right-brain contact – that non-cognitive feeling of connection between people (Schore, 2019). It is also conveyed through reflective listening. This means offering back to the client what the coach has heard.

In the following example, the coach offers back exactly what was said, even using some of the client's words:

Client: He waited until I was on holiday to make his move and get to the CEO.

Coach: He waited till you could not act on your own behalf and approached the CEO.

Alternatively, the coach might reflect back some deeper implied meaning:

Coach: You believe he deliberately manipulated you and also the CEO?

Or:

Coach: It sounds as if you are deeply offended by what you see as a lack of honesty and integrity. (*Here the coach reflects the assumptions and values behind the client's statement.*)

Or:

Coach: You sound shocked and angry. (*Reflecting emotions.*)

Or:

Coach: And as you say that, your fists ball up – did you notice that? (*Reflecting here-and-now embodied experience.*)

Or:

Coach: And as you say that, I notice that I feel scared as well as angry – somehow it isn't safe where you are. (*Offering back a personal here-and-now experience.*) For more about use of self, see Chapter 4.

The aim of the empathic response is to express understanding and support, but also importantly, to deepen clients' awareness of and understanding of themselves – to invite them to listen more deeply to themselves.

Respect

Respect, or what Rogers (1951) called *unconditional positive regard* involves the coach being willing to listen with acceptance and without judgement. Gestaltists talk about *epoche* – the skill of bracketing our own judgements and assumptions and staying with 'what is'. Of course, this is impossible. Human beings are meaning-making creatures and if their childhood upbringing was adequate, they are also equipped with deeply held values by which they make their meaning. We are forming judgements all the time. As psychiatrist and neuroscientist Karl Friston says, our brain's function is 'top–down binding' – recognising patterns, identifying and assessing. Offering unconditional positive regard involves the coach reaching deep into their wise compassion. It calls for an understanding of human fallibilities and capacity to stay curious and at least delay our judging. If we have worked well on our ability to empathise, we should find it easier to be non-judgemental with clients. The difficulty comes when we hear something from a client that really challenges our principles and we find it hard to be open-minded. That is where the third core condition comes in.

Authenticity

Rogers called it *congruence*. It means bringing ourselves fully to the encounter with the client – not pretending to be a blank screen, or an expert, or a 'good question generator', but allowing ourselves to be fully present in all our humanness. This includes all the ways we find ourselves responding to a client moment by moment, which we may or may not choose to express (see Chapter 4). Congruence means, again, having done a sufficient amount of inner work to know ourselves, so that we are fully aware of our responses in the moment, our preferences, our strengths, our vagaries, our sore spots, our 'blind spots', our vulnerabilities.

Congruence does not mean that we will necessarily put our responses into words. However, it means that we do not say anything that is incompatible with our truth, and that sometimes we will be ready to put our reactions and thoughts into words. Hill (2024) discusses 'truth-telling' in psychotherapy and describes Foucault's ideas about *parrhesia* (1983). Hill likens the therapeutic relationship to parrhesia's earliest usage in Greek democracy where the less powerful person speaks truth to power, first establishing a contract for this 'bold speaking'. We might think, quite rightly, that the coach or therapist is the powerful one in the relationship (see Day 2019). However, Hill argues that the contrary is always true also. The coach is the servant of the client and could at any time lose their position if they displease.

There are times when the coach might believe that they have an unpalatable truth (which, of course, can only be *their* truth, not *the* truth) and that it would be of benefit to the client to hear it. In Chapter 4 we will discuss in depth the skill of 'finding what to say and the ways to say it'. For now, suffice it to say that if the first two core conditions are in place – that is, empathic understanding and respectful regard – congruence can be embodied with less fear of offending. The coach does not go 'one-down' and act anxious, apologetic and placatory (which somehow conveys that the hearer *should* be offended) nor 'one-up' as if they are the arbiter of truth and definer of reality.

Example

Coach: As you talk about your colleague, you sound really vengeful and I find I'm worrying about what you might do. Have you got a plan?

The concept of ego states from transactional analysis can be useful here (see Chapter 5). The Child ego state is likely to be full of the adaptations and anxieties learned in childhood. The Parent ego state holds the power and gets to define what is right and true. The adult ego state shares thoughts, feelings and experiences in ways that are appropriate to the situation.

Exercise 2.1

Alone or with a Colleague

Truth-Telling as a Child

What was your experience of saying your truth (what you were feeling, thinking, needing) when you were a child to people in power (parents, teachers, and so on). Were you attended to with interest? Or were you met with anger? Or laughter? Or cold dismissal?

How did the powerful people in your early life wield their power? Might there be a flavour of that in the way you deliver 'bad news'?

Think of a client that makes you feel tired or anxious. What are you not saying to them? Why? How do you imagine them reacting? Are there any echoes?

TASKS

'Tasks' describes the nature of the work of coach and client. If the bond and the goal are agreed between them, it can be easy to overlook the importance of articulating 'how we are going to work together'.

Development, change and growth happen in relationship – with ourselves, with other humans, with our current situation and with the world. When we work with clients, we are interested in drawing their attention to patterns of relating at multiple levels, including with us in our role as coach. We also believe that the present moment contains the entirety of a person's experience if we pay careful attention to it. Therefore, as relational coaches, we are likely to be inviting the client to be aware of themself in the present with us; we will be interested in the patterns of relating we co-create. Are these patterns familiar repetitions of old ways of being, or are they fresh, new and different?

All this might be quite unexpected for a client who expects his coach either to give him good advice or ask good questions. In order to level up the playing field, it is important to check whether the client is ready and willing to work relationally. If they are not, then maybe relational coaching is not for them.

Exercise 2.2

With a Partner

Expectations of Change

On your own, formulate a couple of sentences about your own theory of change. If you are describing yourself as a relational coach, what does that mean to you? Say something about the way you will work with a client and what they can expect from you. Also, what you expect from them, in terms of willingness to look at your relationship together, to learn from what happens in the room together, and so on.

Then, with a partner, practise saying your sentences to a client, making them your own, using your own familiar language so that you can introduce these ideas easily and comfortably.

Even if the client is available to work relationally, the first question will always be about what they expect or hope for from the coaching. The research by Duncan (2014) and his colleagues makes it clear that if the coaching fits with what the client thinks they need, it is likely to be most effective. This doesn't mean that the coach should be a sort of coaching chameleon, trying to be all things to all clients. However, it is worthwhile to find out from the start what the client's 'theory of change' is.

Example

Coach: What made you choose me from the bios you were sent?

Or: What did you see in my bio that made you think I might be right for you?

Or: So how do you think coaching will help this situation of … ?
Or: How do you think I can be most useful?

Questions like these can all be really helpful routes to beginning to negotiate together a shared agreement about a way of working.

GOALS

While research repeatedly confirms that a clear agreement about goals is a prerequisite of successful coaching, paradoxically, the same clear agreement can become a prison. As Einstein is quoted as saying: 'We cannot solve our problems with the same thinking we used when we created them.' If we name our goal today, we have only today's mind to envisage the future, and that does not leave space for the emergence of something new. We see the container of the work – created through relational contact and contracting – as essential so that unpredicted figures of significance may emerge, that go beyond what was imagined at the start. (Sills, 2006). In other words, the agreement about goals needs to balance focus with space and direction with emergence.

Contracting about goals (and indeed tasks), therefore, helps to create a dynamic container for all that lively, real, spontaneous work to take place. A good framework for this kind of work must provide enough clarity to make it safe and purposeful enough for those involved (either as stakeholders or participants or coaches). It must also allow enough flexibility to 'let the main thing be the main thing', as Igwe (personal communication) puts it (Sills, 2012). In other words, it is not uncommon for the direction of the work to change as the client's self-awareness increases. It is important that the contract be flexible enough to allow what is important to emerge.

In the contracting model below, we describe five 'levels' of contracting, one of which is with the coaching client about his goals for the coaching. This level makes use of the Contracting Matrix shown at Table 2.3. It acts as a sort of map of the 'coaching playing field' allowing the work to shuttle between different areas of focus and interest, providing clarity and also freedom.

LEVELS OF CONTRACT

The contract needs to articulate the goals and tasks clearly. And it needs to be congruent with the intent to work relationally, with how things are, and with what we might discover or create, rather than what we wish for or prescribe from the start.

Furthermore, there is another dimension. As coaches, we need to be aware of the aims and goals of our individual client, but we also need to be aware of the wider client 'system,' the other stakeholders and the potentially complex context of the work. Relational coaches need to become comfortable working with the complex question, 'Who is the client here?'.

Figure 2.1 illustrates a model (Sills, 2006, 2012) that aims to account for this complexity. It presents a number of levels, or foci, of contract, along with a number of dimensions. It offers a map, necessarily simplified, but attempting to capture the nature of the coach's task as they address the different aspects of the situation.

Using the notion of levels points to the importance of attending to each type of contract in turn and in order. Our colleague Brigid Proctor (2006) describes this idea through the metaphor of Russian dolls in order to convey the idea that each of the levels of contract is a container for the next.

1. Our Underlying Contract with the world, society, the environment, ourselves.

2. Our agreement with whoever is commissioning the work: The Broad Purpose. Agreements about practical and professional dimensions – The 'Administrative Contract'.

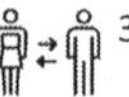
3. The Development Contract. Our agreement with the coaching client about administrative, professional and psychological elements of the contract.

4. The area of focus for the particular session: The Sessional Contract.

5. A mutual commitment of the 'In-the-moment Contract'.

BEWARE THE PSYCHOLOGICAL CONTRACT

Figure 2.1 Levels of Contract
Source: Adapted from Sills (2006, 2012)

Level 1

The Contract that Coaches Make with Themselves

The coach makes a contract – privately and sometimes overtly – with their conscience, their values and their priorities in terms of the world, the planet and society. How often have coaches got deeply into working with an organisation only to find that there is something about its nature or its organisational practices that makes the coach deeply uncomfortable and reluctant to be there? Taking the time to reflect on their purpose in life, the sort of work they are willing to do, any industries they would avoid and practices that they would not condone can be an enriching activity.

When we have done this exercise during our coaching courses, the results are always fascinating. In small groups of three or four, we invite people to reflect on what their values are – what work they would seek, what they would turn down. We then have a large group discussion. There are always some people who name certain industries that they wouldn't work in. Others declare a commitment to social impact. Others refuse to work internally … and so on. And occasionally there is somebody who says they would never refuse any coaching engagement because they believe that the client would benefit from coaching and be a better person in the world.

There is no right or wrong, simply a growing awareness for the coach of who they are as a practitioner and a person – an essential part of working relationally.

Level 2

The Contract the Coach Makes with the Organisation in Which the Client Works

This level is informed by the now well-known work of Fanita English (1975), a transactional analyst, one of Eric Berne's original colleagues who helped him develop his theories. In her simple two-page article, she introduced what she called the 'three-cornered contract'.

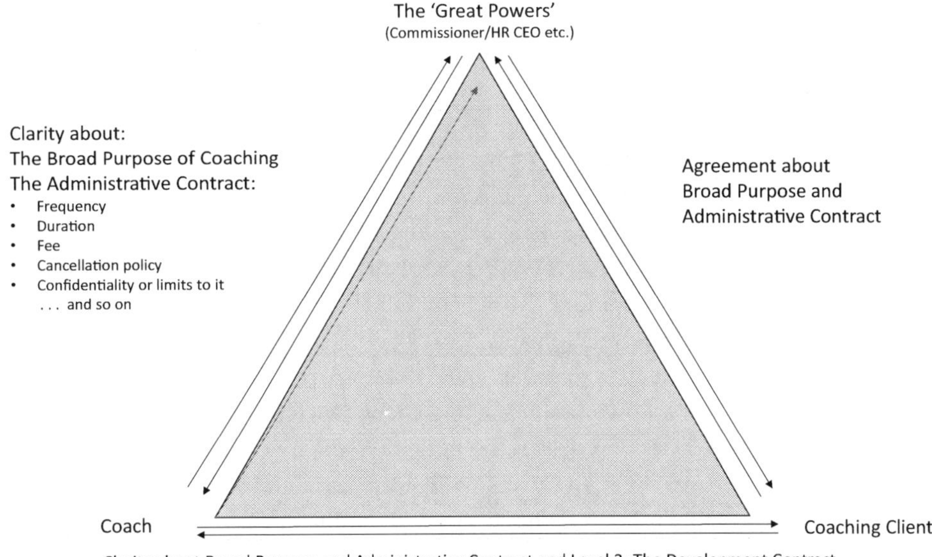

Figure 2.2 The Three-Cornered Contract
Source: Adapted from English (1975)

At the bottom of the triangle is the connection between coach and coaching client. Then there is the connection between coach and the 'Great Powers' as English calls it – in other words, whoever is commissioning and paying for the coaching. This might be the HR Director, the CEO, the client's line manager – or all of them. Arguably, it might also include a coaching 'broker' or the organisation for which the coach works (with its norms and codes of ethics).

Finally, there is the relationship between the Great Powers and the coaching client. English discussed the importance of transparency and agreement on all sides of the triangle. This attends to the administrative or procedural elements of the contract. First, these include the broad purpose of the coaching – for example, transition, talent development, strengthening of skills, leadership development, and so on. This level of contract may also include agreements about:

- Time/place/medium
- Duration/frequency
- Access between meetings
- Fees/cancellation policy
- Confidentiality/limits to (sometimes there might be an agreement from the start for a report on progress or to discuss themes that are emerging in a piece of work with several individuals in the organisation)
- Accountability to third parties
- Recording
- Arrangements for evaluation and review

Tudor (2006) expanded English's model to illustrate the possible multiplicity of power and influence relationships within the organisation. Micholt (1985, 1992) also adapted the model, playing with shortening and lengthening the lines of contact to indicate strength of allegiance and loyalty between parties.

A relational orientation to coaching pays attention to the wider context and system in which the coaching is taking place. From an individualistic perspective, the focus in the mind of the commissioning client can often be on the individual coaching client in isolation, considering the development and change that the individual needs to achieve in order for the coaching to be successful. However, there may be forces at play in the wider system and relationship networks that will have a direct bearing on the individual's capacity for change. Relational coaches can draw attention to this when contracting with the Great Power and coaching client. Once the objectives of the individual client have been considered, they might explore the following questions in conversation with the Great Power and client, where the coach might also offer his own perspectives on the situation and thoughts about the influence of the wider context:

- Now that we have established the goals for the client, are there any factors in the wider context that are likely to support or limit the individual's ability to achieve their objectives?

- What is within the client's zone of control and influence?
- What role might the sponsor of the coaching have in creating conditions supportive of the client's development, such as influencing where the client does not have the authority to do so him/herself?
- Where does responsibility for success lie beyond simply the coach and client?
- In the light of all this, what is it realistic to expect of the coaching, the coach and the client, and do the objectives need to be refined to reflect the wider systemic forces at work?

Clarity in all these administrative areas can enormously enhance the strength and effectiveness of the container along with the client's confidence in it. However, our colleague David Skinner (2012) also points to the inevitable vagaries and complexities of this contract. It is a brave coach indeed who, when working inside their biggest and most important client organisation, refuses to respond to the friendly enquiry from the CEO in the corridor, 'How is the coaching going with Harry?'

Exercise 2.3

On Your Own

Polite Refusals

As with the previous exercise, it can be helpful to compose in advance a couple of tactful sentences with which you can respectfully remind a Great Power that you owe it to them to act with integrity according to the original contract. We are not suggesting any particular form of words because the most suitable ones will be those you choose yourself – and, of course, depend on the relationship you have with the Great Power.

Level 3

The Contract the Coach Makes with the Coaching Client

If the first two levels have been attended to well, the coach and coaching client are then able to enter the coaching playing field together to agree between them such issues as:

- Purpose – the overall reason for the coaching
- Objectives – specific areas of focus for each session
- Methods – coaching models, methodology
- Coach responsibilities – e.g., timekeeping/being prepared
- Client responsibilities – e.g., being open to the relational process

- Style of coaching – e.g., formal vs informal
- Managing the session – coach vs client-led or neither.

The contracting matrix (Figure 2.3) articulates two axes – the vertical describes the range of possible goals, from the measurable and observable (what Berne (1966) called a 'hard' contract) to the intangible and subjective (what Berne called 'soft'). The horizontal axis refers to the degree of self-awareness and insight that the client has. This opens up four types of work that the coaching might involve.

Figure 2.3 The Contracting Matrix
Source: Adapted from Sills (2006)

The client might have:

- A high degree of understanding and a clear articulation of desired outcome – 'I know what I want and what I need to do'. *Behavioural change* contract.
- Clarity about the desired goal, but no idea what is needed to achieve it – or indeed why he hasn't already achieved it. Angus Igwe's (personal communication) 'the main thing is to let the main thing be the main thing' is apt here. Or, 'let the dog see the rabbit'. A *Clarifying* contract.

- No measurable goal in view but an awareness that all is not right and a desire to 'feel better' in some way. An *Exploratory* contact – exploring 'what is'. Here the words of C.S. Lewis (Till We Have Faces, 1956), 'how can they [the Gods] meet us face to face until we have faces', seem to sum up that existential importance of knowing oneself before deciding what we want.
- A clear understanding of what he wants but it is not a tangible outcome. It is described, for example, as a sense of purpose or a need to 'pause on the landing and take in the view'. A *Discovery* contract. This type of contract is summed up in the words of a client who had been on a leadership development course some years before. She said, 'I learned so much about myself. Now everything is fine, but I just want more of myself'.

As circumstances change or understanding develops, the work can move between the four quadrants. Often the client, and indeed the organisation with its eye on the return on investment, will expect the goal to be a measurable outcome, and the broad purpose of the coaching is named as a behavioural change. However, as the work progresses the contract changes.

Example

A client – Michael – recently promoted to divisional leader, discovers that he is expected to present to the board on a monthly basis. He engages a coach to help him make presentations as he has never made them before at that level. The HR Director supports the goal. Early in the first session, however, it becomes clear that what at first seemed a straightforward contract for behavioural change, is much more complicated. This is not a question of learning skills; Michael is seriously incapacitated at the idea of presenting at board level. He feels intensely anxious and is considering resigning from his new role. What is briefly a clarifying contract as he allows himself to really face the extent of his anxiety, settles quickly into an exploratory contract. Michael needs to understand himself and why his fear is so great. He begins to make associations to childhood experiences – an only child at a rough and hostile school – that have left him with evident trauma symptoms.

The coach begins the process of shuttling between an exploratory contract and a behavioural one. As Michael begins to understand and honour his feelings from the past (see Chapter 5) he finds himself able to let go of them, to stop seeing his board colleagues as the punitive and bullying teachers at his school. At that point he is able to engage with some techniques, both for managing anxiety (such as breathing and grounding himself before the presentation) and for making effective and clear presentations.

Exercise 2.4

On Your Own or in Discussion with Colleague(s)

The Contracting Matrix

- To what extent do you already use the contracting matrix implicitly?
- How could you use it to improve your existing contracting process?
- How could you use it to improve your practice in general?

Level 4

The Contract for the Session

Here the Contracting Matrix can be particularly useful as it frames what the client needs in any particular session. Relational coaches develop their own style in relation to sessional contracts. Some choose a structured start to the session, beginning with feeding back on any agreements made in the previous session and getting a clear outcome articulated for the day's session. Other coaches have a more emergent and unstructured style, starting the session with 'What is uppermost today?' or 'What do you want to think about today?' or indeed simply 'What is important?' (Diana Shmukler, personal communication).

It is important to remember that any agreement can be a contract. We simply need to remember that this is what we agreed and be ready to revisit the agreement when the time is right. For example, a client might say, 'I just want to tell you about what I am struggling with at the moment and hear myself talk about it. Then we can see what might stand out.' The coach needs to hold that in mind and at a certain point be ready to return to it: 'We agreed that you were going to just lay out the story here for us both and see where it led you. Where are you with that? Do you have a sense of where you would like to go now?'

What is fundamental is that coaches don't make contracts simply because the rules say they should. We make contracts when *we* need them – to help us focus, to clarify the direction, to contain the complexity.

Level 5

Contracts in the Present Moment

These contracts are the here-and-now negotiation for the immediate next moment. They are a way of re-establishing connection, or respectfully changing the process. For example: 'May I tell you what I have been thinking about?' or 'I have some feedback for you. Are you open to hearing it?' or 'I have a couple of ideas – can I just get them off my chest so they don't interfere with me listening to you properly?' or 'It sounds as if that is really important. Shall we stay with that for a while?' or 'May I tell you my experience at this moment?'

It is not always necessary to negotiate permission to change the direction of the work or to give feedback, but it can be a very effective way of respectfully alerting the client that something surprising might be on its way. It is especially helpful if you plan to experiment with the sort of truth-telling that we discussed earlier.

The Psychological Contract

A hidden dimension of contracts is the psychological contract. We think it was Eric Berne (1966) who first talked about psychological contract. He was referring to an exchange that has two levels of meaning to it – the so-called 'social level' of what is clearly communicated and the 'psychological level' of unconscious communication of something that might be at odds with the social level. This can lead to a sort of unspoken and often unaware 'contract' that can undermine or derail what is explicitly agreed. For example, a colleague got into difficulties with his very senior client when the client said that he wanted a robust, challenging coach:

> Client: I don't want some namby-pamby 'yes-man' as a coach – I am surrounded by that at the office. I want a coach who is going to challenge me.
>
> Coach (whose childhood pattern was that he could never please his critical authoritarian father): Certainly I can challenge ... like this ... like that.

Unfortunately, the psychological contract was something like:

> Client: I think I want challenge but actually I am very unsettled by any criticism, so go gently.
>
> Coach: I must show you how robust I am, but every time I offer a challenge, you push it away. I must try harder, but I know I won't be able to please Dad in the end.

The outcome was, of course, that the coach was fired by a man who believed that people were out to undermine him if they were given power.

Exploring hidden agendas or unspoken expectations – be they personal 'script' or organisational pressures, can go a long way to avoiding collusions or collisions, (Wachtel, 2008) avoidances or stagnation. However, if we work relationally, then these unconscious communications should be welcomed as being a rich source of information for collaborative enquiry. We explore these processes in Chapters 4, 5 and 6.

CONCLUSION

We have discussed the importance of building a strong working alliance between coach and coaching client, creating a relationship in which deep and effective work can be done. Using Bordin's model of goals, tasks and bonds, we have unpacked the elements of this alliance and explored how it can provide a strong container and facilitator of the work, while still allowing creative spontaneity and avoiding rigidity. Where contracting as set out in this chapter is attended to by the coach and coachee, it becomes possible for them to create a field of 'bounded instability' (see Figure 2.4) which contains and balances the human psychobiological hungers (Berne, 1966) for structure, novelty and relationship, and is the place of creativity and change.

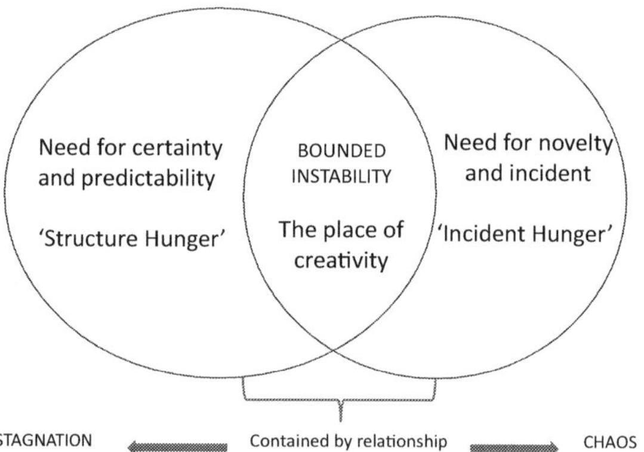

Figure 2.4 The Field of Bounded Instability

We end with a caveat: making a relationship like this is not a one-off event. It needs constant attention to maintain it, as old unhelpful patterns and unexpected misunderstandings arise. When a dynamic happens between coach and client that disturbs the confidence and security of the connection, it is known as a 'rupture' to the steadiness of the working alliance. We shall explore in detail how to attend to these moments in Chapter 6.

Further, given the challenges of organisational life as well as global concerns, increasingly coaching clients bring issues and experiences which cause anxiety.

An important role we have as coaches is to help our clients through the quality and dynamics of the coaching relationship – and ourselves through our own personal work – to regulate any anxiety that interferes with learning and development. We will explore this in more detail in the next chapter.

3 ENQUIRING COLLABORATIVELY

Without awareness, there is nothing – not even knowledge of nothingness.

(Fritz Perls, 1992, p. 31)

MAKING MEANING

Existential philosophy emphasises how as a species we humans are profoundly concerned with making meaning (Spinelli, 2005, 2010). Drawing on this reality, a relational orientation to coaching holds that, as human beings, we are always making sense of our experience in relationship to others. Even when we are alone, reflecting on our experience, this will always involve relationships with others as we experience, perceive, understand and make sense of them in our own minds.

Coach and coaching client bring to the coaching relationship their relative histories, personalities, backgrounds, constructs, beliefs about the world and a myriad of other elements that make up the unique subjectivity of each of us. As we described in the previous chapter, the contracting process and the coach's understanding of coaching methods and methodology set particular parameters and bring a negotiated focus and definition to the coaching relationship and its purpose. Within these necessary boundaries, there remain two 'universes' of individual subjectivity that shape the coaching conversation as it unfolds. On this basis, it can be said that no two coaching conversations can ever be the same.

This relational process makes room for meaning to emerge from the interactions between coach and client. This contrasts with more linear, protocol and competence-based approaches (Bachkirova, 2016); here the coach applies tools, methods and techniques to the coaching client, while keeping his own experience and responses out of the interaction. Both linear and emergent orientations have their place, depending on the context and client requirements moment by moment. But cultivating a capacity for a more emergent orientation is a core component in a relational orientation to practice.

Behaviours and Attitudes Associated with Linear Orientation

- Planning each session and being inclined to stick to the plan irrespective of what the client might be feeling, thinking or saying.
- Having, and being invested in, a clear idea of the direction the client needs to be moving in – a focus on the pre-agreed outcome.
- Having a suite of tools and techniques front of mind to apply to the coaching client.
- Moving to fill silences with a question, model or theory.
- Feeling responsible for getting the client to their stated goals and driving the work in this direction.
- Actively guiding the client in the direction of stated objectives.
- Making decisions about what is relevant in service of the client achieving their stated objectives and calling the client's attention to apparent deviations in order to course-correct.
- Holding the client to account.

Behaviours and Attitudes Associated with an Emergent Orientation

- Holding objectives lightly, bracketing a need for structure and taking time to be present to what the client is saying and how the coach is being impacted.
- Being able to bracket and hold lightly a predetermined sense of direction – to focus on the present moment.
- Being able to allow space for the client to notice, experience and think in the moment.
- Trusting in the process of relating and the fact that insight and meaning emerge from interactions.
- Being willing to consider apparent deviations and meandering as being potentially relevant for the work and for new insight to emerge.
- Valuing and respecting the client's autonomy and right to decide the extent to which he or she may wish to follow through on insights.
- Valuing awareness raising, meaning-making and reflection as fundamental processes in generating insight, shifts in perspective and new possibilities for action.

Exercise 3.1

1. Alone or with a Colleague

Linear vs Emergent Approaches

Reread the descriptions above. Notice which behaviours are more familiar to you.

Do you tend to operate more from a more linear or a more emergent orientation in your coaching?

Is this different with different clients and in different contexts? If so, what might this be telling you about the unique coach, client and context dynamics with each client?

Linear and emergent orientations can be thought of as opposite poles on a continuum. Each has its place and usefulness at different times, with different clients and in different contexts and stages of the coaching relationship. If you tend to operate more from one end of the continuum, how might you experiment with expanding your range towards the opposite pole? How might you hold the tension of linear and emergent so that you can focus on goals while also remaining open to the unfolding and emergent nature of each present moment?

Exercise 3.2

2. With a Colleague

Linear vs Emergent in Practice

Do two 15-minute sessions each of practice coaching.

In one, start by making a clear contract with a measurable outcome. Use this as a guide to the 15 minutes, keeping your focus firmly on the desired outcome.

In the other, experiment with confining your interventions to here-and-now noticings – of your own responses, feelings and sensations; of your client's experience in the moment, including small gestures or movements, the use of particular words, the facial expression, and so on.

THE SUBJECTIVITY OF EXPERIENCE

Relational coaching accepts – and welcomes – the fact of the coach and client having distinct and different subjective experience and realities. It is this principle that makes relational coaching a relationship between human beings rather than an instrumental contract between a coach and coaching client. The instrumental contract sees the coach occupy a clearly defined role where they act upon the client from a place of expert knowledge of coaching theory and technique. In this type of interaction, there is a risk that the client becomes dehumanised or made into an object to be *done to* rather than *related with*.

Welcoming the unique subjectivities of coach and client into the coaching relationship humanises them both. It offers the possibility of a more mutual, democratic relationship in which they both participate. The flow of information and experience between them is seen to be the source of meaning-making, learning and development. This is not to say that the relationship is equal – the very fact that one person is willing to share their concerns and anxieties while the other is there in service of the client's growth means that the relationship is (as Lewis Aron famously said in 1991, p. 33) 'mutual without being symmetrical'.

Bachkirova (2016) contrasts relational practice with the more traditional competency frame for coaching, based on knowledge and skills. Positioning the self in this way acknowledges the complexity and unpredictability of the coaching process which is often missed in more rational, linear and competency-based approaches. It offers a broader approach for clients facing complex challenges as questions regarding their context, role, situation and leadership arise.

Executive coaching clients often bring issues that affect their whole lives. The interventions of the coach emerge not only from an understanding of the client's context, presenting issues, psychological make-up and expressed goals, but from how the coach resonates with all these elements moment by moment (Bachkirova, 2016). In this way, coach and client are in an inter-subjective process of mutual and reciprocal resonance and influence.

WHAT DOES THE COACH BRING?

As we have said before, given the intersubjective, resonant elements of a relational orientation to coaching, it is necessary for relational coaches to invest time and energy in knowing themselves and being aware of what they bring to the coaching relationship. What they bring will inform their subjective experience and resonance with the client moment by moment.

Elements that Inform Both Coach and Client Subjectivities Include:

Age	Gender identity
Nationality	Sexual orientation
Race and ethnicity	Beliefs
Sex	Values

Preferences
Mental models and scripts
Education and training
Life stage
Life history
Personality
Career history
Relationship to power
Understanding of adult learning approaches
Ecological concerns
Political affiliations
Beliefs about and understanding of organisations
Beliefs about economic principles and forces
Social conscience and engagement
Current sociopolitical trends and events
Client organisation, sector and context
Self-awareness
Reflection skills

These elements cannot be spirited away as if they do not exist. We favour naming this from the very start of the coaching relationship in order that it can be explicitly recognised as part of the relational field. It is important that both parties feel able to raise the matter of their similarities and differences, be they a source of interesting learning, or potential misunderstandings or assumptions.

Normally, at the start of coaching there is an initial session where coach and client look each other over and decide whether they want to work together. It may be that the client is meeting a number of coaches in order to choose one the so-called 'chemistry meeting'. Or it may be that the coach has been allocated or recommended. In any case, the coach will be beginning to build some agreement about the goals, tasks and bonds described in Chapter 2. They may ask what made the client choose them, if indeed they were chosen, or they may ask how the client feels about their being allocated. Some coaches may choose not to immediately discuss differences until such time as the topic becomes obviously relevant in the conversation. They believe that naming a difference might imply an over-emphasis on its importance. However, research into cross-racial dyads (Baptiste-Grant et al., 2024) suggests that both clients and coaches believe that talking about racial and other significant differences in identity leads to a deeper, more meaningful conversation.

Many coaches prefer to take the time at the start to share a detailed exchange about their social or intersectional identity. In this way, the client is not being asked to name their concerns or assumptions, they are simply sharing who they are in more detail than is perhaps normally done at the start of a relationship. A middle ground between these two positions is for the coach to make a statement along the lines of:

> 'I am aware that I am a white British woman, raised in a predominantly white neighbourhood, while you are an Indian woman who has lived

and worked all over the world. I am also aware that I am quite a lot older than you. I hope it will be OK if sometimes I ask you what meaning a situation has for you that it might not have for me, and I very much hope you will let me know if I am making assumptions or completely missing the importance of something.'

Relational coaching does not seek an ideal of objective reality but recognises the inevitable subjectivity in all human relationships. It makes use of these similarities and differences to examine how meaning is being made by the coach, the coaching client and in the coaching relationship. Meaning is not seen as incontrovertible truth, but as a momentary way of thinking and perceiving that has implications for how we feel, think and act in the world. Relational coaching also embraces the fact that meanings can only ever be partial; they are prone to evolve as more information becomes available. This can be at once a source of anxiety for those who need to believe in certainty and who associate this with safety, but it also provides creative possibilities for evaluating, assessing and changing the meanings we are making. This is very helpful where it is limiting our potential and capacity for responding to situations.

Exercise 3.3

On Your Own

What Do You Bring to the Coaching Relationship?

Make a list or mind-map of all the significant life experiences, learning and influences that have shaped – and continue to shape – who you are as a person. How do they affect you as a coach?

What assumptions and working models do you have available to you, including theories and skills? Think about how much you lead with these in your coaching as opposed to allowing space for discovery.

CREATING MEANING IN COLLABORATION

From a relational perspective, coaching is seen as a collaborative enquiry process. 'Collaborative' because coach and client work together to explore the meaning the client is making – and the meaning they are making together – about the client's presenting issues, context, needs, focus and new issues, as they emerge over the course of the engagement. One of the things that can surprise coaches moving towards a more relational orientation is how often in supervision with a relational supervisor they are asked about what they are experiencing, feeling and thinking in relation to their coaching clients.

Enquiry emphasises the exploratory and reflective nature of this coaching approach. Instead of following a predetermined protocol, coach and client engage in a free-flowing conversation and the coach pays attention to how the client has formed particular meanings about their situation and developmental needs, what might be potentially limiting their development, and what might need to happen in service of supporting their development. The coach also pays close attention to the meaning he or she is making about the experience of being with the client, and how he or she is being impacted by the content of what is being said, and also the feeling of being with the client, including sensations and emotions. This is because relational coaching pays close attention to the ways in which human beings influence one another's experience in relationship at both conscious and unconscious levels. The relational coach actively works to bring more of what is felt but as yet unacknowledged into the shared relational space of the coaching relationship. This requires the coach to be aware of and reflect on the ways he or she is making meaning, recognise the constructed nature of these meanings and be alert to assumptions and potential blind spots (see the next chapter for a detailed exploration of how to do this in practice).

Cavanagh (2006) describes how knowledge is an emergent property, as opposed to something finite which is either acquired or lost – for example, in forgetfulness. Access to knowledge moment by moment is 'shaped by our relationship to self and other – we can be rendered dumbstruck and lose our capacity to think in

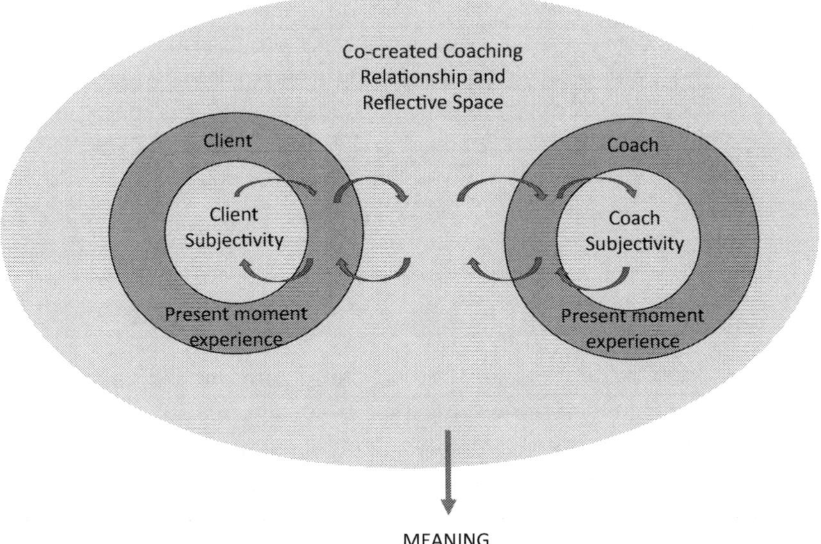

Figure 3.1 Relational Coaching as a Collaborative Meaning-making Process
Source: Adapted from Cavicchia and Gilbert, 2018

a particular conversation where we are being bombarded by questions' (p. 331). With this, Cavanagh is commenting on the potential disbenefit of those coaching approaches that hold that the client has all the answers within them and that the coach needs to draw them out through questioning.

A relational, intersubjective orientation sees knowledge as arising where the subjectivities of coach and client interact; differences can be explored and negotiated. In this way, the coaching conversation is 'an organization that emerges from the complex interaction of the coach and client – it is a co-created conversation' (Cavanagh, 2006, p. 337). This is also the territory of associative intelligence and 'bricolage' – a term coined by Lévi-Strauss (1968) – where new connections stand to be made by combining different realms of knowing and experience. In this co-creation, mental models and theoretical knowledge are brought together and constructed, then emerge informed by the uniqueness of each moment from 'within the complex responsive dialogue that goes on between people and within the person' (ibid., p. 332).

Exercise 3.4

With a Colleague

Dialectic Enquiry

Conduct what is known as a 'dialectic enquiry'. Sit opposite each other with your knees about a foot apart (in other words, close enough to be intimate but not on top of each other). Set a timer for ten or fifteen minutes and commit yourself to the conversation.

Start by sitting in silence for a minute, just being in each other's presence and being aware of what thoughts, feelings and noticings arise in you. Then begin to speak, taking it in turns to share what comes up for you as you sit together. Allow yourself to be stirred and to respond to what your partner says and does.

MEANING IS SOCIALLY CONSTRUCTED

Implicit in a relational orientation to coaching and meaning-making is the assumption that meaning is something that is socially constructed (Burr, 2003; Gergen 1985, 2009). Facts as observable phenomena might initiate the meaning-making process, but different individuals will make different meanings from the same observed facts based on their own subjectivity (Spinelli, 2010). Relational coaching adopts the perspective that meaning is subjective and socially constructed and it is to this process of meaning-making in relationship that coaches give their attention with their clients.

In relational coaching, the focus is not on seeking universal truths or employing past protocols and logic. Rather, the focus is on the process whereby the client constructs meaning in relation to their situation. If the meaning is limiting in some way, it might need to evolve. The coach supports both exploring the meaning-making process and also acting as a catalyst for experimentation with new ways of making meaning and identifying the implications of these for the client's development.

AWARENESS

Many individuals have limited awareness of how they construct and organise their experience moment by moment; they simply take their experience as given. They identify with their own thoughts and take them to be who they are. As such, they operate and behave in a kind of mechanical way, a bit like an aircraft on automatic pilot.

A central skill and orientation in a relational approach to coaching is the cultivation of awareness. In Gestalt approaches to coaching, awareness is seen as crucial to development and increasing awareness of 'what is', is in and of itself a powerful driver in facilitating learning and growth (Perls, 1992). In this paradoxical theory of change as expressed by Beisser (1970) change happens not when we try to be something we are not, but when we fully experience what we are.

Awareness is the ability to observe ourselves and our experience moment by moment with ever-increasing breadth, depth and subtlety. This is not limited to the content of our minds and the thoughts we are having, but includes sensations, emotions, areas of tension or relaxation, movement impulses and how we are taking in information through our five senses. These are considered to be equally (and sometimes even more) reliable sources of information about what is going on in an individual's experience than thinking and thoughts alone.

By enquiring and by noticing cues, the coach helps the client to be aware of what is happening for them, including separating 'real time' experience from our expectations, assumptions and internal commentary.

Without awareness, or with less developed levels of awareness, we risk operating from unexamined beliefs and ideas we have formed about the world, ourselves and others. By raising awareness of beliefs, sensations, assumptions, historical narratives and emotions, we become more able to see the ways in which we and our clients are constructing our experience moment by moment and in relation to particular situations and coaching issues. When we become more aware in this way, it can be said that instead of 'being had by' our experience we now 'have it'.

Relational coaching focuses on exploring with the client the way they are experiencing their current situation and challenges, then constructing development goals as a result. The focus is on increasing awareness of what might be getting in the way of a client's optimal responsiveness to the situation(s) they face. The goal in this orientation is not simply to learn new skills and increase confidence – although these can be useful – but rather to support the client to increase their capacity for self-observation and meaning-making in service of increasing capacity and perspective for responding to their situation(s). When we observe our patterns of thinking and feeling and, as they are now in awareness, test them and evaluate them and understand where they might be holding us back, we can reframe them where necessary. Then we can experiment with new and different ways of thinking and behaving.

As is often the case in a relational approach to coaching, it is as important for coaches to be cultivating awareness in themselves as well as supporting clients to do the same.

CORE ORGANISERS OF PRESENT-MOMENT EXPERIENCE

Ogden and Minton (2000) have developed a very helpful map for supporting us as coaches – and our clients – to cultivate awareness. Drawing on neuroscience research, Gestalt psychology and principles of Hakomi psychotherapy, this map describes the ways in which human beings are constantly organising and constructing their experience moment by moment. This is always happening whether we are aware of it or not.

The map of the core organisers supports clients to develop the reflection skills necessary for many leaders facing complex challenges and uncharted situations where pre-existing protocols are limited. Leaders are thus enabled to relax attachment to fantasies of control and develop the awareness and skill to reflect and respond more creatively to the situations they find themselves in.

Core organisers support the coach and client in noticing what each is experiencing as well as the meaning each is making of the experience, the emotion that it gives rise to and the thoughts and behaviours that flow from it. Once we have awareness of these processes and patterns we can act upon them, we can explore and question our beliefs, assumptions and the meaning we are making from experience, we can evaluate this in terms of its effectiveness and usefulness for the situation we/the client currently find ourselves in.

The core organisers are:

- Cognition
- Emotion
- Five-sense perception
- Movement impulses
- Sensation

These represent five different territories and functions of the nervous system as it responds to stimuli from the environment. They also represent different stages in the evolution of the human brain from the early 'reptilian brain' which deals with sensations, through the later 'limbic system' of emotions and social engagement, and finally the newest part of the brain responsible for registering and representing experience in cognition and thinking, the 'neo-cortex'.

Historically, Western thought has privileged the functioning of the neo-cortex, enshrined in Descartes's famous saying, 'I think, therefore I am'. This is partly because often what most people have greater access to and experience of is their thoughts, and this has led to the erroneous assumption that because we can be aware of thinking, this must be the most important function of the brain (McGilchrist, 2019). Neuroscience research has shown that before we become aware of a thought, our nervous system and other parts of the brain have processed vast amounts of sensory information, which shape the particular thought that arises and we become aware of.

The nervous system processes information entering through the senses in either a 'top down' or 'bottom up' way. Top-down processing refers to cognition leading. Our thoughts, memories, beliefs and the meaning we have made from experience act as maps for making sense of our somatic (bodily) experience and for managing it. 'Bottom up' refers to information and stimuli that move from sensation in the core organisers upwards through our impulse to movement, perceptions and emotions to our thoughts, memories and beliefs.

Both directions are necessary and can be made use of in coaching for helping clients to understand how they are making sense of their experience. Cognitive behavioural approaches, for example, make use of top-down processing, whereas Gestalt approaches focus on exploring body sensations, posture and movement impulses, using bottom-up processing to track the way in which we experience and make sense of experience.

USING THE CORE ORGANISERS TO CULTIVATE AWARENESS

Over-emphasising the role of the neo-cortex means that many of us and our clients have been educated in ways that privilege thinking and logic over a fuller embodied experience. *All* the core organisers are sources of information about how we are experiencing a particular situation or challenge, not just our thoughts. From a relational perspective, we need to cultivate ever-increasing awareness of the totality of our experience moment by moment in order to enquire collaboratively with our clients in service of new discoveries, learning and change.

The map of the core organisers acts as a navigation aid for helping us to discern which of the core organisers we are most in touch with. For many of us and our clients this will be cognition – we will know what we think but may find it harder to know what we feel. For others, they may be more in touch with sensations and have less access or awareness of how they think about their experience. We can then use the map to develop greater sensitivity to those core organisers we and our clients are less able to notice. This must happen first in ourselves as coaches in order to then be able to support this in our coaching clients.

Exercise 3.5

On Your Own

Scanning Your Core Organisers

The neuroscientist Daniel Siegel (2010; 2018) has shown that where attention goes, neurons fire, and that when neurons fire they form and strengthen connections. This proven neuroscientific principle underpins the use of the core organisers. By simply directing our attention to the different core organisers, we are increasing neural firing and the ability of our mind to make new connections.

Take a moment to think of each of the core organisers – cognition, emotion, five sense perception, movement impulses, sensation – and see if you can sense how much access you have to each. Do a scan of your bodymind and see what is figural.

Call to mind a recent pleasurable or enjoyable event or experience. Go back over the experience in your mind remembering as much detail as you can.

As you remember the experience in the present moment, direct your attention to the different core organisers.

What sensations are you aware of?

Spend a little time experiencing these sensations in the body. These may include stillness, a sense of relaxation in the muscles or, if the experience is one of excitement, you might feel some energy building. You may notice how the body moves as you breathe. You may also experience an absence of sensation. Notice what that is like.

As you focus in on any sensations, notice movement impulses, including stillness. Don't immediately put your impulse to movement into action; sit with it and see how it amplifies as you pay attention to it. Later, slowly and mindfully make the action you have felt drawn to and see what arises for you.

Notice what you are picking up through your senses – temperature and movement of air on the skin, sounds, sights, smells.

Notice emotion.

Notice thoughts.

Do the exercise again, but this time think of a mildly challenging situation. Track your core organisers in the same way.

What do you notice?

Warning: a few people, often those who are survivors of trauma of some kind, find focusing deeply into their body to be dysregulating for them. Make sure to notice if you become tense as you do this exercise, or if your client does if you introduce it to them. If that happens, come back to the present and the contact between you.

RIGHT BRAIN TO RIGHT BRAIN COMMUNICATION

Relational approaches and relational neuroscience have demonstrated the ways in which human beings subtly and profoundly shape one another's experience of self and other in relationship (Schore and Schore, 2008; Schore, 2009).

Example: as the supervision group met for its regular meeting, one of the women started by saying that her husband had just received a serious cancer diagnosis. He had little time to live. The supervisee spoke calmly but her voice quavered as she shared her news. The supervisor felt her own eyes filling with tears as she resonated with her supervisee's barely hidden grief and she noticed another member of the group – a big, hitherto unexpressive man – reaching for a handkerchief to wipe his eyes.

Through increasing sensitivity to the core organisers, we can pick up unspoken hints from our clients about what they are experiencing that even they might not be aware of.

While relational coaching makes use of traditional coaching theory such as contracting, focussing on goals where appropriate, asking good questions and so on, there is equal emphasis given to the experience of being with our clients and the processes and dynamics of relating between us. Those processes are full of information about the client, the coach and also the dynamic of the relationship between them. Other factors that might be influencing the client and the coaching from outside of the coaching relationship may also arise (see next chapter for a detailed exploration of these processes and how to make use of them in the coaching relationship). Rather like developing a more and more sensitive telescope for seeing further and further into space, cultivating awareness and using the core organisers allows us to see more and more deeply into the relationship between coach and client.

USING THE CORE ORGANISERS

The core organisers map offers a systematic way to pay close attention to the coach and client experience moment by moment.

The coach holds the map in mind and, with a present-moment focus – i.e., noticing when a core organiser is being expressed as the client speaks, directs the client's attention to it and then invites them to explore others. This approach can be used whenever the coach wishes to raise awareness of how the client is organising their experience and responses in relation to a presenting issue. The coach then tracks with the client what emerges.

The process has three stages:

1 The coach notices a core organiser as it is manifested in the present and gently comments on it – for example, 'You frown as you say that' or 'I notice that you tensed your shoulders just then – did you notice?' or 'I am beginning to feel anxious – are you too?' See other examples below.
2 The coach directs the client's attention to the other different core organisers – for example, 'and as you pay attention to that tightness in your throat, does an emotion come up?' or 'and when you have that thought, what image comes to mind? What do you notice happening inside?'
3 As awareness increases, the coach watches for shifts in energy, emotion, thoughts, insight indicating new learning and perspective. When shifts occur, these are integrated, again using the core organisers.

The more we direct the client's attention to different core organisers, the more we increase awareness and the possibility for change to happen.

Examples of Present-moment Language of Awareness Raising Using the Core Organisers

'What does it feel like now to be telling me about this conversation with your manager?' (sensation)

'As you remember now the difficult conversation you had, do you notice any sensations?' (sensation)

'As you tell me about the responsibility you feel in your new role, your hands move to cover your chest, what is that like?' (movement impulse)

'Imagine you are meeting your new team for the first time. As you hold them in your mind's eye, what do you notice?' (sense perception – visual channel)

'As you imagine now the meeting with your team, is there any emotion?' (emotion)

'As you notice that you feel prepared for the product launch, what emotion are you aware of, if any?' (emotion)

'As you focus your senses on that, is there a thought that comes?' (cognition)

The more we draw attention to different core organisers, we are increasing neural firing in the client's brain. This supports enquiry and discovery, and can raise energy for taking action once a new possibility has emerged, which is very useful if a client is initially not sure about how they think and feel about their presenting issue(s) and what action to take.

REGULATING ANXIETY

Where a client may already be anxious, or where anxiety arises as a result of using the core organisers to enquire, the coach needs to stop drawing attention to the range of core organisers, which will increase energy, and focus instead on settling and regulating the client's nervous system. This can be achieved by focusing on one core organiser only, typically sensation in the peripheral nervous system (see exercise in Chapter 4, focusing on arms and legs where we talk about embodiment) or inviting the client to place both feet on the ground and focus on the sensations in them. These two processes – first, drawing attention to all the core organisers and second, focusing only on one – can be thought of as an accelerator and brake. They help to ensure that the client remains sufficiently engaged for insight to occur, but not so activated in their nervous system that their ability to reflect and enquire is hijacked by anxiety-induced reactions.

Window of Tolerance

Dan Siegel (1999) coined the term 'window of tolerance' to describe the zone of nervous system arousal in which we are able to function and engage with other people most effectively. As a result of our development histories, each of us will be able to tolerate varying degrees of intensity of emotion and physiological arousal. This will vary from individual to individual and in relation to different contexts and events. One coaching client, seeing a frown on his boss's face, may notice a flutter of anxiety and yet be able to remain thoughtful and curious about what might be going on for the boss and continue to engage in conversation. Another client, on seeing his boss frown, might be flooded with anxiety and, imagining that the boss is furious with them, avert their gaze, blush and become tongue-tied. This is described as being outside one's window of tolerance. When we and our clients are operating within our windows of tolerance, we are able to notice our feelings and thoughts in the present moment and make choices about how we wish to respond. When we cannot tolerate mounting levels of anxiety, we lose our capacity for reflection and will react unthinkingly in order to try and regain a sense of safety.

This is because the window of tolerance is connected to the functioning of the autonomic nervous system which has evolved to take swift action in response to actual or perceived threats to our safety. As it is 'autonomic', it functions independently of our conscious thinking processes. An individual's life experience, including trauma, plays a fundamental role in determining the sensitivity of our nervous systems to actual or perceived threat and our capacity to remain in our window of tolerance.

It is possible for coaches to encounter clients with extreme symptoms of trauma and post-traumatic stress. Should this happen, sometimes as a result of a traumatic event outside of the coaching relationship or if some current stress has triggered an old trauma, coaches need to consult with their supervisor on how best to support and proceed with a client. This can include referral to a trauma specialist where required, potentially in addition to, not necessarily instead of, the coaching.

However, given the pressures of modern organisational environments, clients do often display signs of nervous system activation that need to be attended to in the coaching relationship. The autonomic nervous system responds to increased stimulation, stressful experiences and overwhelm in two ways: either by increasing energy via the sympathetic nervous system, as is the case with fight, flight and high freeze responses to stressful experiences, where we would be at the top end or 'spinning out' of our window of tolerance – this is referred to as 'hyper-arousal',

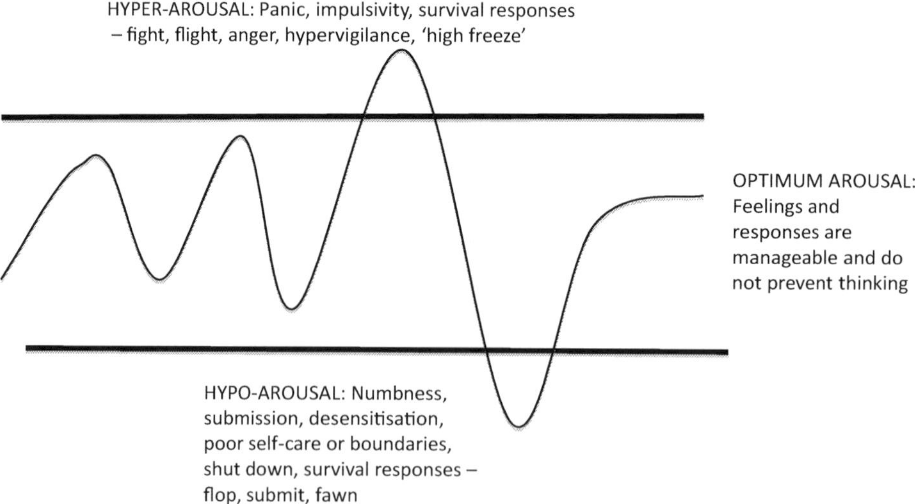

Figure 3.2 The Window of Tolerance
Source: Diagram from Joyce and Sills (2018); Based on Ogden et al. (2006)

or by reducing energy via the parasympathetic nervous system as in flop, fawn and submit responses, where we would be at the bottom or 'dropping out' of our window of tolerance – this is referred to as 'hypo-arousal'.

Both responses result in a number of experiences that affect a coach and client's ability to remain thoughtful, present-moment focused, reflective and responsive. This is primarily because the nervous system interrupts the functioning of the neo-cortex so that energy is redirected to the muscles in the case of hyper-arousal or simply shuts down the mind and body in the case of hypo-arousal.

Effects of Hyper-arousal

- Feeling anxious
- Going off sick
- Having angry outbursts and shouting at staff
- Inability to concentrate or focus
- Reduced ability to notice what is happening, reflect and consider a range of possible interpretations of events
- Automatic assumptions of threat and negative thoughts
- Heightened self-criticism
- Rash and impulsive action

Effects of Hypo-arousal

- Feeling numb
- Absence of any emotion
- Flat energy
- Going through the motions
- Mindlessly doing what they are told
- Inability to think and reflect
- Withdrawal and distancing from others (including the coach)
- Sense of hopelessness and disconnection from resources

Understanding the workings of the autonomic nervous system allows relational coaches to attend to their and their clients' levels of nervous system activation and resource themselves and their clients to remain within or return to their window of tolerance if they have 'spun' or 'dropped' out. This is not only relevant for managing the effects of stress, but also for creating and maintaining conditions in which the client can learn. Where a client is at the edges or outside of their window of tolerance, their capacity to make use of the relationship with coach and reflect on their experience in service of developing new insight and perspective will be reduced or non-existent.

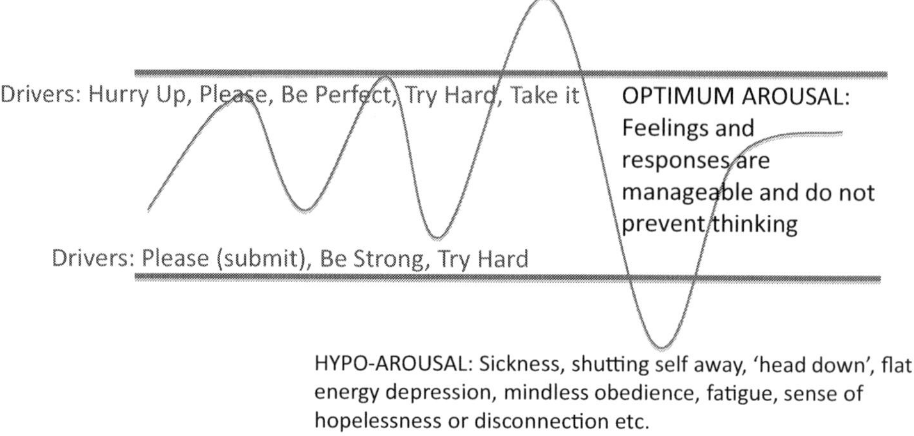

Figure 3.3 Typical Stress Behaviours in the Workplace
Source: Diagram adapted from Joyce and Sills (2018); Based on Siegel (1999) and Ogden et al. (2006)

Supporting the Client to Return to the Window of Tolerance

Resourcing the Client

Where a client is hypo-aroused in the face of overwhelm, the coach can suggest resourcing experiments to support increasing energy such as movement, walking together with the coach in nature, inviting the client to tap their arms and legs to stimulate sensation.

When a client is hyper-aroused, the coach may suggest resourcing experiments intended to reduce energy production in the nervous system. Walking briskly can help to discharge energy, as well as body scans paying attention to the peripheral nervous system (arms and legs), or sensing one's feet on the ground, taking some deep breaths and lengthening the out breath relative to the in breath. So called 'butterfly tapping' (the client crosses their arms across their chest and alternately taps one shoulder or upper arm and then the other) is also effective.

As with all experiments, these need to be negotiated with clients to discover what the client can tolerate or feel comfortable with. As we are all unique, each of us will have or can discover strategies that work particularly well and others less so. The coach can be a useful resource in discovering the different ways the client can learn to regulate energy and remain in their window of tolerance.

Social Engagement

It is important also to remember the role of the coach and the coaching relationship in helping coaching clients to regulate their nervous system arousal. Being in the presence of a coach who can remain in their window of tolerance, think and communicate calmly and clearly when the client might be feeling anxious, can have a profound effect on enabling the coaching client to regulate their own nervous system.

Behavioural Drivers

Clients who enjoy using models and theories might find a model from transactional analysis useful to help them monitor their stress levels and functioning. It is the concept of Behavioural Drivers, first developed by Kahler and Capers in 1974 and elaborated by Kahler (1975). Under stress, trying to avoid anxiety, we often *stop feeling and thinking* to engage in our familiar Driver Behaviour. The drivers are:

- Be Perfect
- Try Hard
- Please
- Be Strong
- Hurry Up
- Take It (more recently discovered by Tudor, 2008)

What happens is that the qualities that are usually our strengths become knee-jerk reactions and we act as if our survival depends on us behaving in this way.

- Excellence becomes paralysing perfectionism.
- Perseverance becomes 'hamster-wheeling'.
- Friendly cooperation slides into mindless pleasing.
- A sense of responsibility turns into shouldering everything and burning out.
- Speed and multitasking becomes agitation and inability to complete.
- Entrepreneurial thinking becomes self-serving pushiness.

The effect of Driver Behaviour is not necessarily catastrophic for an organisation – indeed, it might be relying on its employees for that very behaviour; it may be the organisation's 'cultural Driver'. The damage, however, will be that in addition to being unhealthy for the individual, it is an old familiar pattern, so, by definition, nothing new and creative can come out of it. When the organisation needs to respond to a changing landscape, 'doing what we've always done' is only going to 'get us what we always got'.

It is important for our clients – and ourselves – to get to know our 'Drivers', both when they are the strengths and qualities (sometimes called 'working styles') that are part of our successful way of being in the world, and also when under stress they become signs of our being at the very edge of our Window of Tolerance (see Figure 3.3). Coaches can help clients to recognise their signs and become familiar with the triggers. That way, they can pause to think and find other ways of regulating their anxiety and then choose what they want to do. Gradually over time, the capacity of their window of tolerance can be increased.

Mindful Awareness

An important element here, which can appear counter-intuitive when set against linear and directional approaches to change, is that by becoming more aware of how we are organising our experience, we are increasing our capacity to notice and experience what **is**, which in turn can result in shifts in mental and emotional state, and perspective. As such, working with the core organisers provides a way of deepening awareness in service of change.

As mentioned earlier, the process of increasing awareness is in and of itself a powerful enabler of change. Once we and our clients become more aware of how we are constructing our experience moment by moment, the assumptions behind our actions, or the meaning of a particular niggling anxiety, it becomes easier to see what the best next step might be in service of our development and growth. For example, identifying anxiety and its sources can lead to exploring what forms of support might be needed by an individual to reduce anxiety. It will allow them to take a step into a new territory of being and acting. Surfacing a limiting belief about the consequences of a possible course of action (such as believing that questioning authority will lead to dismissal) allows for the belief to be acknowledged, its origins understood, and for it to be reality tested in the present situation a client finds themselves in.

CONCLUSION

Cultivating awareness is the cornerstone of a relational approach to coaching and the process of collaborative enquiry. Without awareness, coach and client will be limited by existing and familiar patterns of thinking and acting. With increased awareness, the relational coach can pay closer attention to not just the verbal content of the coaching, but also the felt sense of being with the client. All experience is treated as 'potentially relevant' by the coach. Focusing on the different core organisers increases and deepens awareness of a situation. In terms of the paradoxical theory of change, increased awareness supports the emergence of new possibilities.

Research shows that real change happens when, with our prefrontal cortex firmly online (in other words, in the present, in awareness) acting as compassionate witness, we allow ourselves to experience some of our old pains and patterns. Exploring the core organisers in the way described above, is a very powerful way of achieving this.

4

USE OF SELF

THE EXPLICIT AND THE IMPLICIT

Whenever people come together, there are two levels of relating happening: the 'explicit' – the content of their conversation, their internal thoughts and their overt communication. There is also the 'implicit' – the feeling of being together, which is felt but not yet articulated.

Relational coaches pay attention to both the explicit and the implicit dimensions of the coaching relationship and the relationship between the two. The coach listens to their own experience and makes intentional use of this in service of the coaching client's learning and development, including relevant and appropriate self-disclosure.

This chapter contains:

- An overview of the field of 'self-disclosure'
- An introduction to the 'use of self' as the heart of relational encounter
- A four-step process for using the self within the coaching relationship
- Some thoughts about how to develop these skills.

In Chapter 3 we described how, in a relational orientation to coaching, coach and client interact from a place of their individual subjective experience, informed by their histories, psychological make-up, and a host of other factors including values, education, training, career, politics, gender, ethnicity, identity, etc. All coaching is inevitably and implicitly informed by these factors. Relational coaching intentionally makes use of these elements in service of the client's development. A central skill and practice of this approach is the coach's self-disclosure. This can be to do with the coach's experience outside of the coaching room as well as their moment-by-moment experience inside the room with a client. The self-disclosure can be inadvertent or consciously chosen by the coach.

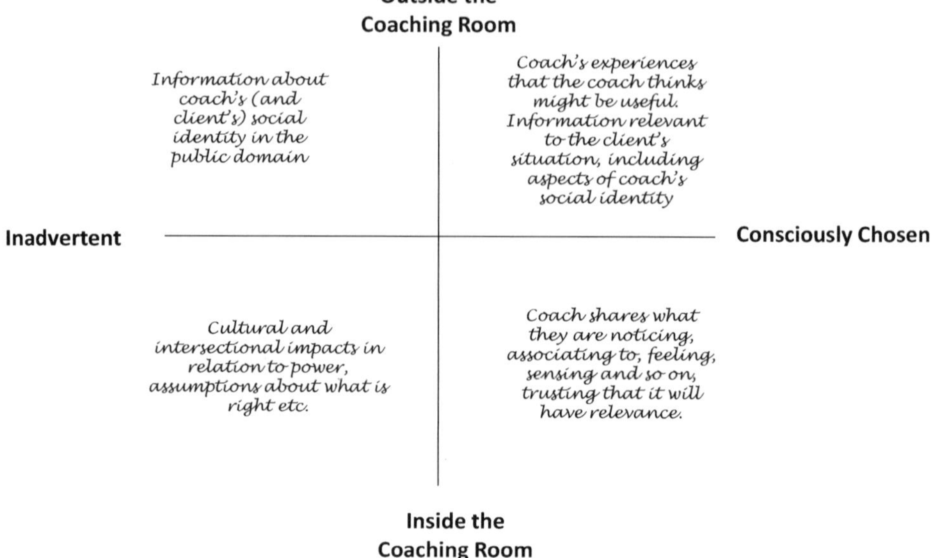

Figure 4.1 Domains of Self-disclosure
Source: Adapted from Joyce and Sills (2023)

Joyce and Sills (2023) have developed the matrix shown (Figure 4.1) to describe four types of disclosure based on the axes of whether the material is located inside the room/outside the room and inadvertent/consciously chosen disclosure.

Outside the Coaching Room – Inadvertent

Coach and client may know things about each other based on available information in the public domain. A client is extremely likely to have put their coach's name into a search engine in order to discover more about who they are, and vice versa. This knowledge will be part of their evolving relationship and inevitably influence and shape the relationship between them. It can lead either to greater transparency between them, or it can lead to misunderstandings and assumptions.

Example

Psychotherapist Aaron Balick (2014) has written extensively on social media, his initial interest sparked by an early incident with an insect. If you search (e.g., Google) for 'man finds huge venomous centipede behind his TV', you will see the story, which was well covered in the media at the time and is still there – for eternity it seems. The story is straightforward – indeed, the headline says it all: Balick heard an odd noise and discovered a very large centipede, which turns out to have escaped from a neighbour's exotic pet collection. However, it had a surprisingly big impact on one particular client for a variety of reasons. While most clients were generally amused or surprised at the discovery, one individual was particularly disturbed as he discovered it by Googling Aaron while he happened to be in a distressed state. Instead of finding the familiar therapist that he knew (and was seeking for a sense of safety), he found an unfamiliar version of his therapist who had a life that was not shared with him, and who, he gathered, had been in danger.

Balick explored the consequences of this event in a clinical paper (2012) (https://link.springer.com/article/10.1057/pcs.2012.19) which he later developed into a book (2014).

Inside the Coaching Room – Inadvertent

Coach and client cannot help but reveal to one another aspects of their cultural and intersectional backgrounds in how they interact, what they focus on, how they think together about presenting issues. Their differences in terms of gender, ethnicity, age, accent and so on will influence the relationship dynamics in both unconscious and conscious ways. As we described in Chapter 3, a relational coach will be likely to name much of their own intersectional/social identity and also to share whatever other aspects of their unique identity is relevant to them. They will invite their client to do the same. Although this will not remove the myriad ways in which both people unconsciously reveal themselves in how they 'show up', it is likely to open a space – to give permission – for these to be spoken about, when either party notices something of interest or significance.

Outside the Coaching Room – Chosen

The coach may choose to share aspects of their experience from outside the coaching room where this is considered to have relevance for the work. If a coach has a particular area of expertise, they may ask the client for permission to share their perspective, if they have something to offer the client in thinking about their presenting issues.

This type of informative intervention needs to be offered in service of the client thinking about their own options and possibilities for action, not as an instruction or with an assumption that the coach knows best. Some purist non-directive coaches will refrain at all costs from giving advice or sharing their experience, not wishing to slip into the role of mentor or consultant. We believe, however, that there is a place for it. Withholding potentially valuable ideas or advice seems to breach the principles of relational coaching where both people are bringing themselves to the encounter.

The only absolutely essential corollary is that it is even more important than ever at those moments for coaches to watch for and monitor the impact of their intervention. What happens to the client? Do they 'swallow whole' the advice without thinking about it? Do they metaphorically – and often actually – close their mouths and refuse even to breathe in while someone else's opinion is in the room? Do they immediately look anxious/annoyed/patiently impatient, and so on? All this is important data for the developing relationship and probably the client's issues (and the coach's).

A particular form of sharing one's opinion is known as psycho-education. The coach might decide that to share a model or some information about human behaviour that they think will help the client feel more confident in the coaching or in planning their course of action. Some clients, perhaps especially those who can only feel safe if they can fully understand and take charge of their own process, really appreciate being shown a model or being given an article to read. For example, some of the accessible models from transactional analysis (see Chapters 5 and 6) have been found hugely useful by clients. Data from research soothes sceptical clients who might think that reflection on self is self-indulgence, or convinces busy performance-driven managers who have no time for the apparently pointless task of making contact with their staff. Information about discoveries in neurobiology can be transformative in helping people understand their relational experiences.

Example

Steve was baffled by his coach's interest in his embodied experience – the feelings and sensations he had in what Fritz Perls called the Inner Zone of Experience (Perls et al., 1951). He was intrigued when she explained:

> It may seem odd that I am asking that when this seems like an issue we should just think carefully about. But the truth is that there are just as many nerves taking information to the brain, as there are taking information from it. The two communicate constantly. If we work only with the head, we run the risk of tensions that are stored in the body continuing to send messages of distress to the mind … long after we think we have settled the matter.

Inside the Coaching Room – Chosen

Here the coach closely tracks how he is experiencing the client and may choose to share feelings, thoughts, intuitions, etc. as they arise, trusting that these will have potential relevance for the client. It remains the client's responsibility and right to discover what, if anything, they can make of the coach's disclosure.

Exercise 4.1

On Your Own

Social Identity Mapping

Choose a client whom you see as different from you. Do an intersectional map of both your social identities. (As an example, look at Figure 4.2, although you may add as many categories as you want.)

How might your evident differences have impact on the relationship? Have they been spoken about? What parts of your social identity do you choose to disclose? What can you not hide?

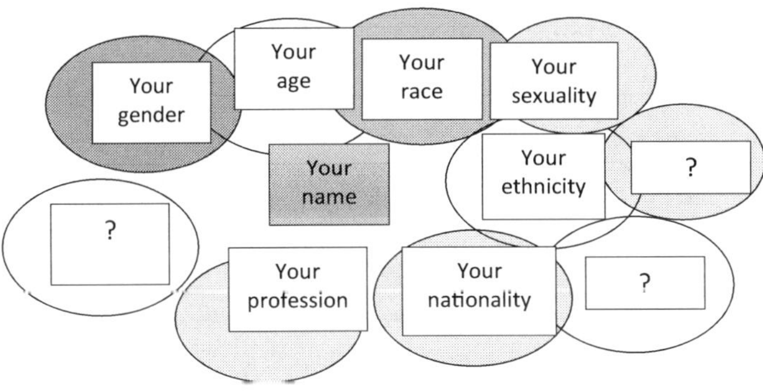

Figure 4.2 Social Identity

Relational coaching takes account of the ways in which human beings are constantly relating in a flow of 'mutual and reciprocal influence' (Stolorow and Atwood, 1992, p. 18) and makes intentional use of these processes to inform the way coaching is conducted. How individuals relate, what is spoken and conscious between them, as well as what is felt that is *not yet* conscious, contribute to shaping how coach and client interact, how their minds shape one another, their feelings, thoughts and how new meaning can emerge for both in this process.

The coach's subjectivity is central in a relational orientation to coaching and fundamental in how a coach collaborates with the client to explore their presenting issues and to make meaning about the client's context and patterns of thinking in order to create new perspectives and possibilities for action.

In the world of coaching and consulting, this is sometimes referred to as 'use of self as instrument'. Here, the coach is thought of as making use of his or her feelings and thoughts to be an instrument of change. From a relational perspective, this is problematic. Coaching of that nature can only be a form of instrumental intervention and risks manipulation of the client in keeping with the coach's agenda.

In a relational orientation to coaching, we do not believe that the coach acts upon the client from a place of superiority or expert knowledge. It is the case that coaches will have specialist knowledge about coaching processes and skills, but these are to be made use of in the context of a collaborative relationship; the coach does not presume to know what the client needs or needs to be.

Within a relational framing of coaching, we prefer simply 'use of self ' or 'use of self-experience' to point to the fact that the coach's feelings, thoughts and sensations provide a potentially rich source of information about their responses to the client, the client's experience (including thoughts and emotions) and the nature of the relationship between them, as well as the context in which they are working. If these responses can be noticed and thought about together, they provide a well of information and meaning to expand both coach and client understanding and perspectives about the work that is taking place between them.

While mutual and reciprocal influence has long been observed and understood in the fields of psychotherapy and psychoanalysis (Gilbert and Orlans, 2010; Cavicchia and Gilbert, 2018), neuroscience has further demonstrated the ways in which human beings shape one another's experience in relationship. The Boston Change Process Study Group (2010) in particular have researched the ways in which, when human beings interact, their historical ways of relating along with dynamics and manner of their interactions have a fundamental and profound role in shaping feelings, thoughts, their construction of reality and the behaviours that follow.

They identify two levels of interaction which occur in all helping relationships. The first is the 'explicit relational' level which represents the content of what is being talked about. This includes goals, thoughts, concepts, assumptions, perceptions, beliefs, descriptions of events and situations, along with observed reactions and responses the client has made to these. At the same time, coach and client are also relating at the 'implicit relational' level. This refers to the felt level of relating – the felt experience of being with one another in the present, including the sense and quality of connection that coach and client experience when working together. This has a dynamic quality and can change moment by moment. Whereas the explicit level is conscious (both coach and client are aware of what they are talking about and what they are thinking together), the implicit level of relating does not happen in conscious awareness. This means that clients and their coaches will also be interacting on the basis of the unconsciously felt experience of being with one another. This will be informed by each of their individual experiences of relating throughout their lives and the unconscious maps they have formed about how to be with one another in human relationships, what contributes to feeling safe and welcome, or anxious and concerned (see also Chapter 6).

Iain McGilchrist (2019) eloquently describes these levels of consciousness as he discusses the two hemispheres of the brain. Both hemispheres think and feel, but while the left hemisphere is associated with more conscious, focused, instrumental thinking – how to manipulate the world – the right hemisphere is devoted more to implicit knowing, pattern recognition, 'big-picture' thinking and feeling, and empathic connectedness. It is also involved with music, imagination and creativity.

The implicit level of relating is the territory of non-verbal communication, facial expressions, tone of voice, how coach and client respond energetically to what is being said and to the ongoing flow of their interactions. A coach whose body language and tone of voice might communicate some mounting anxiety, or who unconsciously converts anxiety into rushing to be overly 'helpful' when a client brings an issue both find challenging, will affect the quality of the relational field with the client. The client may sense that something has shifted in the quality of the relationship at the implicit level without necessarily consciously making sense or understanding what is going on. They may then respond unconsciously by pulling back slightly in the face of the coach's reactions and suggestions. The coach's shift in body language, energy and tone, based on their anxiety, may be picked up unconsciously by the client as a sign that what they (the client) are talking about is problematic or threatening in some way. This, in turn, may evoke anxiety and feelings of self-consciousness or shame in the client.

Given the dominance of explicit thinking in coaching and organisational life, these shifts may not be noticed at the conscious level, and yet they will have significant impacts on the dynamic of the coaching relationship. If a coach can learn to pay attention to these processes and shifts, it becomes possible to name them and think about them with the client.

For example, to continue the above scenario, the coach might be able to share that they have found themselves feeling anxious and wonder aloud if this might be saying something about how the client might be feeling about their situation. In this instance, the coach is making use of the process of countertransference central to psychoanalytic and relational transactional analysis approaches to coaching, where the coach's feelings and experiences are considered to hold information that is potentially relevant to the client, and the context and content of their work, as well as the coaching relationship. The coach may own and name that their anxiety might also be affecting the relationship. This may allow the client to notice their response to the anxiety, that they felt perhaps suddenly confused or anxious themselves. This, in turn, may allow both to reflect on what this anxiety entering the relationship may be pointing to in terms of the context in which both are working. They may notice that the organisation culture is competitive and critical of people who do not appear to know instantly what to do. They may then be able to acknowledge that the client is facing a number of challenges that they have never experienced before and they need time and space to reflect and identify strategies and responses that they feel able to act on.

As a result of noticing more of the implicit aspects of the relationship dynamic, coach and client are able to make meaning from their experience, reset their relationship and recontract for how to be together in a way that is more likely to be supportive and useful to the client. In relational coaching, we take seriously the fact that coach and client are involved in a process of making meaning together about the client's situation and their relationship to it in order to discover new appropriate and effective ways of responding.

Whenever coach and client are able to notice the subtle elements of the implicit level of relating and think about them, as in the example above, these experiences enter the explicit level of relating, generating new insights, understanding and contributing to the developmental narrative that coach and client are involved in creating together. The research of the Boston Change Process Study Group (2010) has demonstrated that being sensitive and open to noticing the implicit relational level of relating and then thinking about it, and making meaning from what is happening at this level, is a fundamental process supporting change and growth in helping relationships. Central to their theory of change is the need to be able to weave together the implicit and explicit. This is seen to be the mechanism whereby clients can increase in awareness and understanding in service of developing broader perspectives and expanded repertoires for action.

Exercise 4.2

On Your Own

Focusing on Sensation

Think of a coaching relationship you are currently involved in. When you think of your client, what do you notice, sense and feel as you hold them in your mind? How does your body feel – tense, relaxed, neutral? What do you sense is the quality of relationship between you and your client? Is there a recent interaction that has stayed with you? What happened between you, what feelings and thoughts come to mind as you remember it?

Given the centrality in a relational approach to coaching of paying attention to both the explicit and implicit levels of relating, the coach's use of self, their experience and how they might make use of their experience in service of the client's development is a fundamental skill to be cultivating and developing.

DEVELOPING THE ABILITY TO 'MAKE USE OF SELF'

Clemmens (2011) describes four components involved in making use of self in the context of psychotherapy: embodiment, attunement, resonance and articulation. These have been further expanded upon in the context of coaching (Cavicchia and Gilbert, 2018).

Embodiment

This is the experiential quality of the coach experiencing themself as a 'full self' as opposed to a 'role self' or 'pretending' in order to be seen as they would like to be seen' (Yontef, 2007, p. 21). We can achieve this by becoming present to the breadth of our experience in the moment. Clemmens (2011) suggests that we might notice our breath, feel our feet on the ground, notice the quality of our muscle tone in our bodies and faces, paying close attention to how we are orienting ourselves in relation to the client. These will be different in different contexts and with different clients moment by moment. Clemmens stresses that 'all of this process needs to be an ongoing discipline and as figural as my thoughts or theories about the client and our process' (p. 42).

This can represent a radical shift for many coaches who may be inclined to focus at purely the cognitive level of interaction, asking questions and deploying techniques, processes and tools to elicit discovery and movement towards the client's originally stated goals. While this aspect undoubtedly has its place, embodiment is the first step to becoming more present to oneself in relation to a client and bringing more of oneself to the encounter.

Many practitioners and writers have reflected that presence is central to the practice of embodiment: the coach's state and orientation to the client. Silsbee (2008) stresses that the coach's way of being is fundamental to their ability to produce genuine new shifts, insights and behaviours with clients. Nancy Kline points to the relationship between coach presence and the capacity for thought in the client – 'the quality of a person's attention determines the quality of other people's thinking' (Kline, 2002, p. 17). Fogel continues in this vein by discussing the value of 'slowing down and being in the subjective emotional present' (Fogel, 2009, p. 23). Sills et al. (2012) describe presence as 'being in the here and now, ready to be alive to every facet of the moment' (p. 103). It is characterised by an aware sensing into oneself, being authentic, maintaining non-attachment to specific outcomes and attuning to the client and their context (Denham, 2006). It involves holding a tension between simply noticing experience and also being oriented towards a client's development and the relevance of what is arising for this objective. Chidiac and Denham-Vaughan describe this as 'fully being while doing' (2007, p. 11). In this process the coach moves between 'grace' as a quality of receptivity to what is experienced and 'will' in the form of directed action or taking initiative in service of the client's learning and growth (Denham-Vaughan, 2005). There is an echo of Gilchrist's (2010) elaboration of right- and left-brain hemisphere function here. This form of presence includes the knowledge and information the coach brings to the relationship as a latent resource which may be called upon in different ways depending on what emerges between coach and client. The coach's objective is to be present and available to being impacted by the client moment by moment, and as responsive to the needs of the situation as they can be (Chidiac and Denham-Vaughan, 2007). It requires holding the tension of the polarities of receptivity and activity.

Embodiment requires that the coach is willing and able to sense more into his or her direct experience moment by moment with each client. It involves learning to sense and notice more the quality and locations in the body of different sensations, levels of energy and movement, impulses. We find the theory of core organisers (Ogden et al., 2006) which we described in the previous chapter useful here in supporting embodiment and helping coaches differentiate between sensations, movement impulses, how information is coming to them through the different senses, emotions and thoughts. Embodiment is the gateway to tuning the self to be able to make use of the relational impacts between coach and client in service of meaning-making.

Neuroscience has demonstrated that where attention goes, neurons fire. And neurons that fire, wire together (Siegel, 2010). This important discovery points to the fact that by focusing our attention on different parts of our bodies, neurons associated with these areas fire in our brains. As they fire, they wire together forming more efficient neural networks. If we focus on a particular pleasant sensation, this can become anchored and more available to us through the process of neurons associated with this sensation firing and wiring together.

Psychologist and expert in neuroplasticity, Rick Hanson (2011) points out that humans are wired to notice the negative and dwell on it as a way of surviving. But, he says, we tend to let go of good experiences too quickly so they don't support the myelination (the formation of the myelin sheath around a nerve to allow for improved conduction) of positive neural pathways. He encourages us to linger over the memory or current experience of a happy or enjoyable event, feeling the emotions, images, sensations and movements that are linked to that good experience – gratitude or peace or joy, and so on. We should hold on to that embodied experience as long as we can – for at least 10 seconds and ideally up to 30 seconds, and this helps to 'hardwire the brain for happiness'.

These neurological processes underpin Gendlin's (1997) work on focusing and sensorimotor psychotherapy's (Ogden et al., 2006) building well-being processes that describe how it is possible to train ourselves to become more sensitised to and aware of our sensations.

Exercise 4.3

On Your Own

Developing Capacity for Embodiment Body Scan

There are many exercises that coaches can make use of to cultivate a greater capacity for embodiment. For embodiment, exercises that encourage moving attention through different parts of the body and sensitising to different sensations are particularly useful. These exercises are referred to as the 'body scan'. With the explosion in mindfulness over the last decade, there are many resources that can be accessed online, along with a range of apps that provide exercises that coaches can make use of. The following link will take you to an example of these resources, but there are many out there and you may experiment and choose whichever appeals to you most (www.youtube.com/watch?v=e0f9wa2SUX0).

A simple introduction to sensing different parts of the body, focusing on the peripheral nervous system, which, for those new to this way of working, tends to be less likely to evoke intense feelings, is the following:

Find a quiet place to sit where you will not be disturbed for about 10 to 15 minutes. (It is best to try to stay awake for this exercise, so sitting on a chair rather than lying down is preferable.)

Begin by checking your posture. It can be helpful to move away slightly from the back of the chair you are sitting in and ensure that your spine is elongated so that it can support your upper body.

This exercise can be done with your eyes closed. If, however, you prefer to keep your eyes open, then it is best to relax your gaze and focus it downwards at 45 degrees on a single spot on the floor for the duration of the exercise.

Next, bring your awareness, the focus of your attention, to your breath. Notice where you most are aware of your breath. This might be at your nostrils or at the back of your throat. You might also feel the rising of your chest on the in breath and the falling of the chest on the outward breath. You may notice the breath deeper in your body with the rising and falling of the belly.

Take a few moments to simply focus on following the movement of your breath wherever it is most noticeable to you.

Then, letting go of the focus on the breath, bring your focus to your right foot. Make yourself open to noticing whatever sensations you experience in this area. There may be a tingling, a pulsing or an absence of sensation. If you don't feel anything, then simply register the sensation of absence. You are not hunting for sensations, but simply being aware and present to whatever your experience is in the present moment.

Then, at your own pace, begin to sense up your right leg, the shin, the calf. Again, simply opening to whatever sensations you encounter here, including the absence of sensation. Continue to sense up your right leg until you reach your right hip joint.

It is very normal and inevitable in an exercise like this to become distracted by thoughts, worrying, trying to make sense of what you are experiencing, maybe even striving to make something happen, wondering if you are doing the exercise correctly. Whenever you become aware of having become distracted in this way, simply acknowledge the distraction, without judgement, and bring your awareness back to the part of the body you are focusing on. We cannot prevent these distractions, it is simply the way our minds work. However, every time we become aware of a distraction and bring our attention back to the body, we are developing a capacity for greater presence and embodiment. Over time we can steady our focus and support greater connection to the body.

Then, letting go of the focus on your right hip joint, bring your awareness to your right hand. At your own pace, sense your way up your right arm, starting with your wrist, then the forearm, the elbow, the upper arm until you reach your right shoulder.

On reaching your right shoulder and noticing any sensations you experience here, bring your awareness to your left shoulder. Now repeat the process of the right side of the body, this time in reverse. Sensing down your left upper arm, through the left elbow, the left forearm, wrist and left hand. Then, letting go of the focus on your left hand, bring your awareness to your left hip joint. Then, sensing your way down your left thigh, knee joint, calf, shin, ankle, until you reach your left foot.

Finally, letting go of the focus on your left foot, expand the field of your awareness to include the feeling of both arms and both legs. In doing this, you are moving from a narrow focus to a wider focus of attention, which is also a useful skill to practise and supports taking in more information than is usually the case with a narrow perspective.

When it feels right for you, letting go of sensing into your arms and legs, open your eyes (or lift your gaze if you have been looking at the floor) and bring your awareness to noticing the sights and sounds of the room you are in.

Practising this exercise, ideally daily, over time, supports developing greater capacity to tune into our bodies and the more subtle experiences that can contain much information of use to our own meaning-making and the meaning-making of our clients.

Attunement

Through cultivating a sense of embodied presence the coach is able to attune more to the client. Attunement involves the opening or reaching out with our senses to whatever experience arises, resonates, echoes or shifts within us and our client. This requires the coach to be at least in part rooted in tuning into their own felt experience while including the experience of the other in their awareness.

The part of the previous exercise, where you were invited to expand your focus from the left foot to sensing both arms and legs mirrors this process of opening our senses to include not only our inner experience, but also noticing how we are experiencing being in relationship with our client.

Exercise 4.4

On Your Own

Developing Capacity for Attunement Body Scan

Repeat the body scan in the above exercise, ending with sensing both arms and both legs.

As you slowly open your eyes, rather than rushing to connect with sights or sounds, practise letting these come to you. Try to keep a portion of your attention rooted in the sensations of your arms and legs as you open to the different stimuli coming to you via your senses. Some people find it helpful to think in terms of 60 per cent of your attention rooted inside yourself and 40 per cent focused on the different stimuli coming to you from the outside.

How do you experience this? What do you notice? What happens to your sense of connection to yourself if something captures your attention? Can you become aware of the process of moving from inner attention to outer attention? As you pay attention to the outside, what happens to the sense of connection to the inside and vice versa?

Though initially challenging, this practice will support coaches to become more focused on their body sensations as they are impacted by the client and cuts across the tendency in many coaches to leave their connection with their bodies and focus their attention and energy in thinking. This is similar to tuning an instrument. If we take the idea of use of self seriously, then we need to practise increasing and maintaining our sensitivity to being impacted at the levels of sensation and emotion as well as cognition as we sit with and interact with our clients.

In relational practice and use of self, the coach will shuttle between inner experience and outer awareness as well as noticing the dynamic and the meaning that is arising between them and the client.

If a coach's attention is predominantly located in the realm of thought, listening to content, reflecting logically about what they are hearing and scanning their memory of strategies and exercises, they will have less attention available for deeper listening and tracking of their own subtle responses. Attunement supports coaches to enter into a receptive mode and open to noticing what subtle and not-so-subtle shifts are occurring in clients and in themselves. Clemmens (2011) stresses that in 'order to do this we must empty our task-oriented mind and allow our bodily experience to be part of the foreground' (p. 42). With attunement, the goal is awareness of how the coach is being impacted by the client and also inviting the client to become curious about their sensory experience in relationship with the practitioner and the context.

Resonance

Building on attunement, resonance is where we notice our own movements, breathing, posture, subtle sensations, emotions, tentative associations and fleeting images in relation to the client, and stay present and open to what we notice as we are impacted at a bodily level. This 'staying with' allows what is emerging in us to become more developed and to unfold. Clemmens compares this to being a bowl or resonant instrument (Clemmens and Bursztyn, 2003). This is an embodied form of empathy where we experience being touched and impacted by the client and where our own experience is shaped in this process (Joyce and Sills, 2018).

Exercise 4.5

On Your Own

Resonating with Your Clients

Think about your current client case load. Scan through all your clients one by one. Notice which clients immediately come to mind and which might be harder to get a sense of. See if you can sense into each client and the quality of your relationship and relationship dynamics. Does anything stand out particularly with each client (including the possibility that with some clients what stands out is the fact that nothing stands out)?

Things to look out for that might stand out with different clients (this is not an exhaustive list):

- The client's body posture
- The client's tone of voice
- The client's levels of energy: flat/animated/moving between the two
- What the client talks about and what is not spoken but felt
- Feelings of congruence or incongruence between what the client talks about and how they are talking about it
- How open and available the client is to being in relationship
- How the client responds to the coach's interventions
- The coach's levels of energy
- Any images or metaphors that come to mind for the coach about the client, the coaching relationship or organisation context (even if they don't make sense initially)
- The coach's levels of interest in the client
- The coach's levels of internal support and resilience: resourced/doubtful?

- The client's levels of interest in the coaching
- Quality of collaboration
- Level of mutuality or hierarchical transacting
- How engaged the client/coach feels
- Any particular sensations or emotions that arise in the coach in relation to the client
- Any particular assumptions or thoughts that stand out in the coach's mind about the client and their situation

As you notice what does or does not stand out for you with each client, take a moment to 'hang out' with your experience of each particular client. See if you can notice the impact of what stands out for you on how you feel and think about this client and the work you are doing together.

Resist the temptation to make what you are experiencing quickly fit into your existing models for understanding your client, bracket pre-existing assumptions. Once we have attributed meaning to a particular experience, we can become very attached to it and then confirmation bias leads to only noticing data that fit with our hypothesis.

How might you be more tentative in relation to the sense you are making? What assumptions are you making that might need to be held lightly to enable more noticing? Practising intentionally, cultivating an attitude of tentativeness or 'holding hypotheses lightly' in this way can support coaches to bring this attitude to the moment-by-moment interactions with their clients.

Articulation

Articulation is the process whereby that which is resonating forms into thought, language or gesture. Aspects of our sensory experience might unfold and amplify, and may then give rise to a specific image, thought or association, to a memory or theoretical perspective. It is the process whereby we put our experience into meaning through our own thought processes and then articulate this to our client in gestures, words and statements.

Embodiment, attunement and resonance are closer to implicit modes of relating, whereas articulation moves into the explicit domain where experience is connected to language and thought. Earlier, we set out how change and transformation happen through the interplay of both implicit and explicit domains, and the four practices of embodiment, attunement, resonance and articulation allow coaches to move between these two domains while inviting their clients also to do so. This process corresponds also to John Heron's (2001) hierarchical model of the human psyche where sensation and affect (feelings) give rise to the imaginal realm of experience, which includes the imagery of imagination, memory and perception. The next dimension is the conceptual domain of thought, reflection and language. Here our experience is translated into beliefs, assumptions and propositions about ourselves and the world which inform our practical action. Reflection is also mediated through existing guiding principles, assumptions, beliefs and theories. How these guiding principles arise or not is important to consider.

As coaches, we need to be able to draw on all our life experience and learning to date. This is not about 'dredging up' experiences, but rather being open to noticing what arises and 'floats' in as we listen to and are impacted by the client. This is in keeping with Cavanagh's (2006, 2013) view, which we discussed in the previous chapter, that knowledge is not a static thing but rather the experience of knowing emerges in dialogue and in relationship. This represents a radical departure from ideas about the coach's presumed neutrality and detachment. With relational coaching we are explicitly acknowledging and embracing the territory of intersubjectivity and collaborative meaning-making. The coach cannot be neutral in how he or she is impacted but can aim to be neutral in attachment to any particular emerging thought, perspective or action.

It is very common and understandable that when we start our coaching training we tend to hold on a little tightly to what we have been taught, be these processes, protocols and specific skills. We can then lead with these as opposed to allowing space to notice more of what is arising in us, our clients and the coaching relationship. In order to work more relationally, we need to notice when we are holding on a little too tightly to a tool or model to allow more space for thoughts, possibilities and insights to emerge. In practice, we often move along a continuum of leading with pre-existing ideas, theories and practices, and the opposite orientation of slowing down, allowing

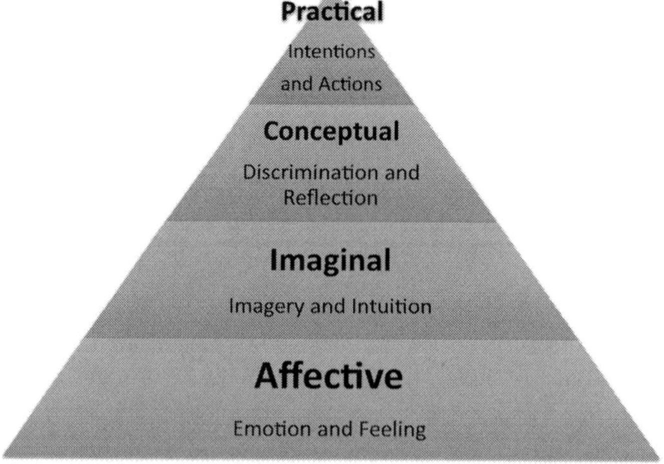

Figure 4.3 Heron's Hierachy of Ways of Knowing
Source: Adapted from Heron (2001)

space for noticing more and creating conditions for meaning to emerge from the relationship dynamics and dialogue between coach and client.

When practising articulation, we listen deeply to the richness of data entering into the shared space between coach and client. We cannot help but notice and select certain aspects that capture our attention based on the filtering of our own experience, emotional responses and energetic attention. This is also the time to be paying attention to what might be missing, avoided or not being said – the practice Western (2012) refers to as 'minding the gap'. We pay attention to the feeling tone of what the client is saying and the feeling tone it elicits in ourselves. Cavanagh (2006) describes how

> 'the client's communication enters into the coach's personal reflection space. Here it continues to interact with the coach's experience, mental models, emotions personality, history, and so on, and we begin to see patterns as the client data elicits ideas, images, metaphors and theories. Meaning or knowledge begins to emerge for us in this process. This processing often continues post-session and during the coach's supervision'
>
> (p. 339)

Articulation is the process of making known either to ourself or the client the embodied shifts happening in the coaching relationship as we sense them (Clemmens, 2011). The form, manner and timing of our articulation has to take into consideration the client's levels of resilience, maturity, cultural and linguistic register, patterns of interaction, functioning, stage of the relationship and field conditions.

A useful orientation here is the Gestalt principle of 'possible relevance' (Parlett, 1991, p. 70). Here all experiences that arise in the coaching relationship can be considered to be potentially relevant. This supports coaches and clients alike to hold an attitude of open curiosity, exploration and experimentation with whatever is arising in the course of their dialogue. This spacious approach which allows for possibilities to emerge is not as random as it may sound. The relationship of the coach and client is held and shaped within the context of the contract, the client's goals and the organisation in which they are working. At the same time, it can be very useful and support creativity to be open to noticing more of the implicit, and be curious about feelings, thoughts, images, memories that arise for each. Having said that, as coaches we also need to hold in mind aspects of the client's story, themes, context and stated goals when considering what to disclose or draw attention to. We track closely how implicit bodily experience and explicit cognitive processes are intertwined.

As coach and client explore and make meaning together, the coach might experience memories, sensations, images, theoretical lenses entering into their awareness. Where this experience resonates or persists in some way, it is possible that it is pointing to something of potential relevance to the coaching process with this particular client. It is important that the coach is able to think about and reflect on what is arising for them in the context of the work with each particular client.

The coach may develop a working hypothesis based on this, but the coach cannot presume to know whether what they are experiencing is relevant until they share their experience and test this with the client. In this respect, it is crucial that the relational coach making use of themself needs to cultivate the ability to hold thoughts, meanings and hypotheses lightly.

From a relational, intersubjective perspective, the inevitable subjective differences between coach and client are seen as a vital and necessary source of learning potential. Stacey et al. (2000) have identified three factors that contribute to a free-flowing and generative conversation:

Connectivity – referring to the need for rich and meaningful themes, what in Gestalt are referred to as 'figures of interest' (Leary-Joyce, 2014).

Anxiety – as an inevitable component when one is faced with the unknown, and meanings that are emergent rather than predetermined. Too little anxiety and the conversation loses energy; too much, and anxiety shuts down thinking (as was seen in earlier chapters).

Diversity – which supplies necessary novelty for new meaning to emerge. Coach and client will hold different perspectives and it is these differences that provide the essential levels of misunderstanding and cross-fertilisation needed to stimulate new connections between experience, ideas about experience and to generate new insights.

Articulation of any difference needs to be offered in a spirit of collaborative enquiry. It is important here that as coaches we resist any pull to become attached to what we are noticing or the meanings that are emerging. There is a risk that our own anxieties about being seen to be clever, experts, insightful, value adding and successful can also get activated here and we can find ourselves prematurely wedded to a position. As with all interventions where we are articulating a sensation, perspective, memory, image or thought, the attitude of 'hinting' applies (Phillips, 1998). Hinting is an attitude or orientation, not a practice. A hint can only ever be taken, not given. If we think we can give a hint, we are inevitably caught in a linear and deterministic exercise of pressuring the client and pushing for a particular direction or outcome.

The Language of Hinting and its Function

In order to be able to 'hint' at possibilities and offer difference in a way the client might be able to make use of, we must first ensure that we are genuinely unattached to our thoughts and ideas about what is going on or may need to happen. There will be times when this is easier and times when it is more challenging.

If we are invested in being right or in thinking we know what is best for the client, the language we use will ring hollow. There will be an incongruence between the words at the explicit level of relating and the implicit relational field. The language of hinting needs to communicate the non-attachment of the coach and allow space for the client to pick up or reject what is being offered depending on what resonates for them, if anything. Examples include:

- I don't know if what I am about to say will be of any use to you, but I find myself wondering …
- I am not sure where this is coming from but I feel …
- Do you think it might be possible that … ?
- How does what I have said land with you?…
- I don't know if this is right but I find myself remembering …
- This might be a bit bonkers but see what happens if you consider …
- I am not sure where this is coming from – if it makes no sense to you just ignore me …
- I don't know why but where I have gone with that is …

Hinting works both ways. The coach, listening closely to the client might pick up on a particular use of language, notice what is not being said, sense incongruence between narrative content and the client's body process and emotions. These signs can be thought of as unconscious hints from the client as to how they are organising their experience and meaning-making. In turn, the coach articulates their own response to what they are hearing which, equally, can only ever be a hint at some latent possibility that only the client can choose to pick up on or not.

Coaches need to track closely the impacts of their gestures and articulation with each client moment by moment. They need to remain alert to when a client might be overly compliant and quick to pick up everything a coach says, or equally, when a client might appear overwhelmed, distracted or distant as a result of experiencing the coach's intervention as interfering in an unhelpful way.

Cavanagh (2006) describes the freshness of this form of knowledge generation where coach and client can enter into a mutual and generative conversation fuelled by the diversity of their individual subjectivities: 'The knowledge that is elicited is new knowledge – we coaches see it in the connections between what the client is experiencing and our own experience and understandings. When we are truly engaged in the conversation, this emergent knowledge has the character of insight, rather that the mechanical overlay of our pre-existing models on the client's situation. It is an 'aha' experience (Lewin and Regine, 2001). Yet the insight is tentative until shared and agreed' (Cavanagh, 2006, p. 339). Any articulation or intervention on the part of the coach is an informed experiment, the offering of a possibility, to discover what use, if any, the client can make of it in their context and in service of their learning, knowledge generation and the broad parameters of the contract.

The coach's role is to contribute to creating conditions in which this might happen. Through articulation and sharing their perspectives, based on inner experiencing and reflection, the coach 'puts this transformed data back into the shared space for ongoing consideration ... the client then picks it up and, all going well, takes it into the crucible of his own internal dialogue' (ibid., p. 339). The conversation continues in this way until coach and client have developed together enough shared understanding, or shared mental model, that opens up the possibility for new and differently informed action on the part of the client. This way of working is more in keeping with a post-modern orientation to coaching where assumptions about expertise and authority are less certain and taken for granted. Cavanagh (2006) also cautions against the coach becoming too identified with or wedded to a perspective – as might happen if the coach is overly identified with being an expert –

> 'when our theories and models move from being perspectives that nourish the conversation to the necessary conclusion of that conversation, they have moved from being information to ideology. When this happens, we as coaches have moved from a stance of curiosity and service to one of coercive arrogance'
>
> (ibid., p. 342)

Or as one of our supervisors puts it: 'it is very difficult to have a good conversation with someone who knows what they are talking about!' (Wainwright, 2016).

In making use of self, Bachkirova (2016) suggests that the coach needs to understand him-/herself; maintain, look after him-/herself; continue to monitor and reflect on him-/herself in order to ensure the quality of the instrument. Placing the use of self as central to a relational dialogic approach to coaching means that depth of practice comes for the depth of the practitioner. Bachkirova (2016) suggests that in order to engage our depth we need to practise:

Looking in – Understanding our inner nature, our histories and their shaping of our present moment interactions. Embracing the role of the whole organism in our actions alongside thinking and logic.

Looking out – Engaging with concepts and theories as well as the external ideologies, beliefs systems and discourses that shape our minds. As we mature as practitioners, we also need to become more and more aware of these ideas and hold them lightly so as not to become too wedded to any particular view.

Developing as a relational coach who makes use of self is a lifelong learning journey requiring commitment and ongoing reflection. It is not a set of once-and-for-all acquired skills. This reflects the evolving nature of meaning-making, learning and knowledge.

Bachkirova (2016) uses the term 'competent self' to denote the version of coaches that is rooted in a competency model of coach development and practice, and, 'dialogic self' to denote that version of coaches who bring more of themselves to the work and work relationally.

Table 4.1 The Conditions for Good Use of Self (adapted from Bachkirova, 2016)

Conditions for developing use of self	Why?	What and how?	Where/when?
Understanding yourself	Ensuring congruence between you and your approach	Learning what you experience and understand as yourself and how it changes	Personal reflection, coaching, psychotherapy, spiritual practice
Looking after yourself	Sustaining energy and preventing burnout	Appropriate lifestyle, making time and space for restoration, nourishment, nurturing	Any appropriate place, time and frequency
Monitoring quality of use of self	Checking for self-deception, confirmation biases, over-attachment to particular ideas, theories, habits and bad habits	Developing as an individual and practitioner. Understanding the nature of self-deception	Self-awareness, self-reflection, regular supervision and continuing professional development

Source: Bachkirova (2016) (adapted)

Table 4.2 Comparison between Competent and Dialogic Selves of Coach

Aspects of coaching	**Competent self** *Competency-based training and approach of coach*	**Dialogic self** *Relationally oriented coach*
Role of the coach	Expertise at least in the processes of coaching	Partner in dialogue
Skills and tools	Are the main assets of the coach; can appear instrumental and not attuned to the client's experience moment by moment	Are available but secondary to the collaborative engagement and meaning-making; skills, tools, techniques arise contextually out of the ground of relational connection
Concerned with	Good practice, effectiveness and impact	Collaborative meaning-making in the session
Coaching relationship	Is a means for successful work – e.g., the development of sufficient trust	Is an end in itself – a model and crucible for collaborative enquiry out of which new insight and possibilities of action emerge
Communication is	Dialectic – dealing with the explicit meaning of statements	Dialogic – attending to the implicit meanings and intentions behind words as a communication from one human being to another
Aiming for	Resolutions and action points	Not aiming for specific outcome or closure, can appreciate the value of issues remaining unresolved, embraces emergence and expansion of perspective leading to more choice, creativity and flexibility
Potential limitations	Excessive structures and frameworks can stultify the process and reduce innovation and creativity	Coaching process without structure can move around without benchmarks for progress

Source: Bachkirova (2016) (adapted)

Exercise 4.6

On Your Own or with Your Supervisor

A Process for Use of Self with Clients

Working through the following steps after a session in reflective notetaking and/or during supervision can develop our capacity to pay attention to how coach and client influence each other and how meaning emerges in relationship. Over time, using these steps to guide our reflections retrospectively increases our capacity to pay closer attention to these processes moment by moment with clients.

- What do you see, hear or observe in your client/relationship?
- How are you impacted – sensations, emotions, movements?
- What thoughts and tentative meanings arise?
- Is there a theory that comes to mind that further illuminates?
- What happens if you intentionally look at what you are seeing and experiencing through a familiar theoretical lens?
- Are you able to intentionally shift theoretical lenses in order to look at what you are experiencing from a number of different perspectives?
- On the basis of this further meaning-making, what do you feel inclined to do next?
- What is your intention?
- What do you do on the basis of the intention (including doing nothing)?
- What happens next? Remember that the meaning of the coach's intervention/gesture is revealed in the client's response (Mead, 1934/2015, 1967).

Exercise 4.7

With a Colleague or Learning Partner

Listening to your Unacknowledged Responses

Think of a coaching client:

- What is it that you would like to say/disclose to the client, but feel that you can't? Write it down.
- What is it that stops you from saying it? Discuss this with your partner.
- What does it say about you? What might it mean about the client, their context and the relationship between you?

CONCLUSION

In this chapter we have outlined some perspectives on 'self-disclosure' – the coach sharing with the client their personal thoughts, feelings, associations, experiences. We looked at when it might be appropriate to do this, as well as ways of sharing views or experiences so that the coaching client doesn't feel dictated to or manipulated.

We then explored deeply what it means to fully commit to a relational process, to trusting what is co-created in the coaching encounter and exploring together what both people's deepest embodied responses might mean for the work.

5
THE PRESENTING PAST

We have talked a lot about the importance and the vibrant reality of the co-created, emergent here-and-now encounter – the 'sloppy work', as the Boston Change Process Study Group calls it (see, e.g., BCPSG, 2007), that is intrinsic to novelty and creativity, rather than the rehearsal of past ways of being. And yet, every psychological approach to understanding human beings recognises that the past influences the present, that early in life people develop patterns of relating to self and other, and then have a tendency to repeat those patterns. The different theories have different terms for this phenomenon – for example: 'repetition compulsion' (Freud, 1914, *Erinnern, Wiederholen und Durcharbeiten* – 'Remembering, Repeating and Working-Through'), 'organising principles' (Stolorow, 2013), 'enduring relational themes' (Jacobs, 2017), 'fixed Gestalts' (Perls et al., 1951), 'life script and psychological games' (Berne, 1961), RIGS – 'representations of interactions that are generalised' (Stern, 1985).

Neuroscientist and psychiatrist Karl Friston (2010) explains this phenomenon as a product of the function of the brain. He describes how we are bombarded by sensations from the five senses and from the body, which he calls 'Bottom up', chaotic, free energy. The brain's job is to 'minimise surprise' by recognising patterns – called 'Top-down binding' – which is predictive processing based on pre-existing models. Friston calls the brain an 'inference engine' which organises our experience of the world to ensure that our predictions become self-fulfilling prophecies (Vasisht, 2021). When the brain makes a prediction that isn't immediately borne out by what the senses relay back, Friston believes that it can minimise free energy in one of two ways: it can revise its prediction – absorb the surprise, concede the error, update its model of the world – or it can *act* to make the prediction true. In other words, the person acts in such a way as to maximise the chances of getting the same reactions from the environment as they received in the past.

In psychotherapy and coaching, this process of the coaching client bringing archaic relational expectations into the present and acting towards others as if they were figures from one's past is called 'transference'. The response that is evoked in the coach is called counter-transference. Of course, this simple explanation implies that the transference is one way only. In reality, of course, in a relationship of two subjectivities, both people are transferring patterns from the past and eliciting a response in the other. The ensuing relational dance is bi-directional and so gives rise to the term in more relational approaches of 'co-transference'.

However, the brain is alert for anomalies. They cause ambiguity and in that moment of ambiguity our internal working models are revealed and can be revised. This is the process that is at the heart of relational coaching. In the present moment, coach and coaching client can become aware of, and potentially question, old assumptions as they emerge in transferential interactions. It is the magic of what Pat Ogden calls 'relational alchemy'. As the coaching conversations unfold, it is almost inevitable that at some point the coach will say or do something that is an enactment – a repetition – of a distressing encounter in the past that causes a rupture in their working relationship. This is the opportunity to pause, practise 'radical openness' (Hart, 2018) and carefully explore the rupture, where the coach can own their clumsiness or affirm their understanding of the client's feelings and create an ambiguity that might lead to a new neural pathway. This is known as rupture and repair (Safran and Kraus, 2014).

THE CYCLE OF SCRIPT

The Transactional Analysis concept of life script refers to an enduring story-like life pattern with interconnecting themes that are unique to an individual (Berne, 1961; Lapworth and Sills, 2011). The 'script system' or 'script cycle' model (Sills and Salters, 1991) describes how experiences and meaning-making in childhood lead people to develop habitual ways of feeling, thinking and acting that reinforce and maintain those earlier patterns of meaning-making. These patterns (the themes of the broader script) are not impervious to change, but they may be resistant. The script system offers a simple map of this process of maintenance as a cycle divided into four sections, shown schematically in Figure 5.1.

In the figure, Sections A and B belong to the past; Sections C and D describe the here and now. Sections A and D concern external, observable processes; Sections B and C concern experiential processes that are not directly observable.

(A) The sequence begins with the early developmental experience as the young child's developmental needs for safety, structure,

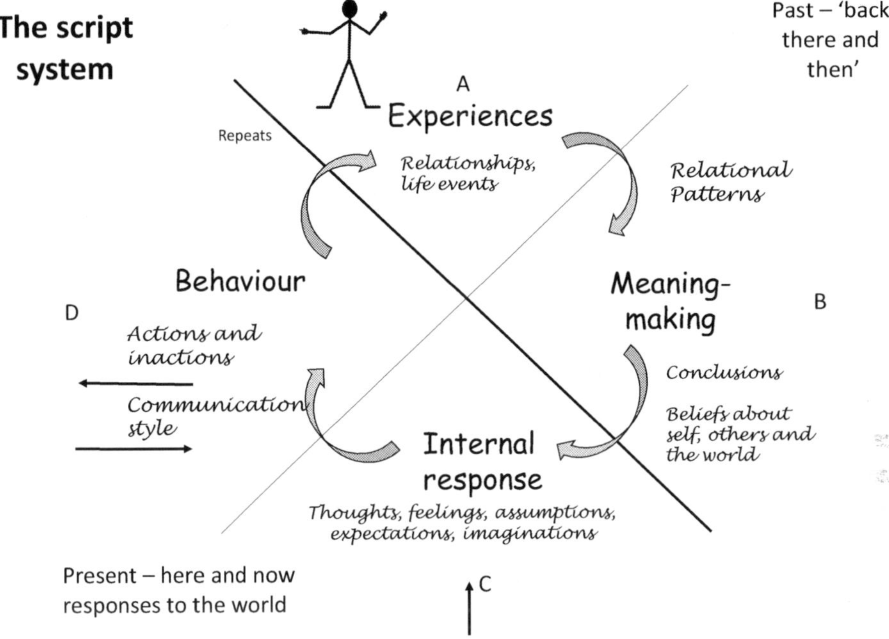

Figure 5.1 The Script System
Source: Adapted from Sills and Salters (1991); Lapworth and Sills (2011)

incident, relationship and agency are received and responded to by the environment. This is known as 'script protocol' (relational experience) and Section A includes the subsequent partial repetitions and re-enactments shaped by culture, family and chance that create an echo of the original scene.

(B) The internal counterpart is the meaning-making that emerges from the experiences described in A. It includes adaptations and unconscious decisions about how to get needs met enough to survive not only physically but psychologically and emotionally. The power and resilience – or rigidity – of the life script reflect the frequency and intensity of the experiences.

(C) Once a life script has been formulated in (B), it can be reactivated by events bearing a similarity to those in (A). It is manifested in the form of internal beliefs and processes that can become problematic to the individual.

(D) The consequent external manifestation of the script represents the individual's observable behaviour based on the reactivated script.

A life script is not a closed system. The individual can assimilate new information and thereby update his or her beliefs (Section B). However, coaches often need to focus on the problematic elements when a script system of thinking, feeling and behaving has become a closed one, limiting new learning and options. The script system model was designed for reflection and intervention in such instances. The coach can address any of the four sections in a spirit of collaborative enquiry in order to see how the client's past might be presenting in the coaching space. They can also use it as a way of gathering together what they know about a client and taking stock of how they have been working with them. Which of the sections have they been focusing on? Which might they have missed?

It can also be very interesting to draw up the script system of the client's organisation. Organisations too have early experiences and meaning-making – often influenced by the script of the founders – be they entrepreneurs, family members or socially minded governments. Patterns of behaviour become habitual – 'this is the way we do it around here' – and certain feelings and ways of thinking are amplified while others are 'disappeared'. The organisation's script is also influenced by its primary task, so that a firm of accountants might develop patterns about attention to detail, a social media firm is all about creativity and a firm making baby products had a tendency to nanny its employees. A client can usefully reflect on whether their organisation's script reinforces their personal one or whether it is at odds with it, which might explain, for example, a client's difficulty in fitting in (see also Chapter 9, Relationship and relating as a moral imperative, pp. 123–135).

Working with the Past in the Present

This chapter has a strong theoretical component which we think is necessary for understanding the ideas of working with past patterns in the present. In order to maintain the focus on skills, we have included a detailed case study to bring the theory to life.

Example

Colin, a 39-year-old male, had first come to see me (CS) at the suggestion of his HR director to understand how Colin's behaviour in the workplace had contributed to his being overlooked for promotion to positions for which he was ostensibly the best candidate. When I met him, we identified his lack of proactivity on his own behalf and his general air of disinterest in life, both personal and professional. However, I realised that this absence of vital connection went deeper than a failure to achieve promotion and I suggested that Colin might like to engage in some psychotherapy to explore this. Colin was reluctant to see a therapist; he had tried counselling before and had felt confused and inadequate with his therapist. When he asked whether we could explore together in the coaching, I agreed.

Our first session was spent getting to know each other and attempting to identify Colin's goals for coaching. I say, 'attempting' because apart from understanding his lack of promotion, he seemed not to have any desires for himself. As we talked, he described a life devoid of passion and stimulation; he couldn't remember feeling differently, although he was aware of feeling 'a bit depressed' when he saw that other people 'seem to have more fun than me'. Gradually, however, he began to get more curious and interested in the notion that somewhere along the line he must have lost his zest for life. He acknowledged that in theory, being a normal baby, he must once have experienced feelings and desires. What had happened to them? He began to like the idea of 'having more of myself', so we agreed to work together, initially for ten fortnightly sessions, first to clarify what the issues might be and then to explore them.

As a way of creating a working alliance, I invited Colin to talk about whatever was on his mind or interested him. His rather flat affect and ponderous manner – although in his late 30s he seemed much older – made me fairly sure that it would be an unusual experience to have someone listen and attend to him with care and attunement, and I hypothesised that this would be essential in his establishing a sense of 'self in relationship' that felt more juicy and vital. In terms of the domains of transference (Hargaden and Sills, 2002; Joyce and Sills, 2018), I was thinking about the 'introjective transference' – the provision of the needed relationship. I was also aware that our similarity of culture (we were both white, British) and age (I was probably his mother's age), meant there was ample room for the *projective* transferential relationship to flourish.

We mainly worked in the here and now together, largely because Colin had a tendency to lose himself in verbiage. However, I invited him to tell me about his early life, as I almost always do when working with a client's relational behaviour. Using the Script System (Figure 5.2), I was able to put together a picture of how his passive presentation developed.

Section A: the early experience: Colin had been born to a mother who suffered from depression, especially after giving birth. By the time Colin was born, his older brother was already eight years old and Colin had almost no memory of him. There had been two pregnancies between the first and second sons, but both had miscarried in the second trimester. Colin's father was away on business most of the time.

Colin's earliest memory was of being in the lounge; night was falling but no one had put the lights on; his mother was sitting motionless in a chair and he was 'playing' on the mat, though he didn't remember having toys. He remembered being a bit older and looking out of the window at the other children playing in the street. He had not been allowed to go out to play because his

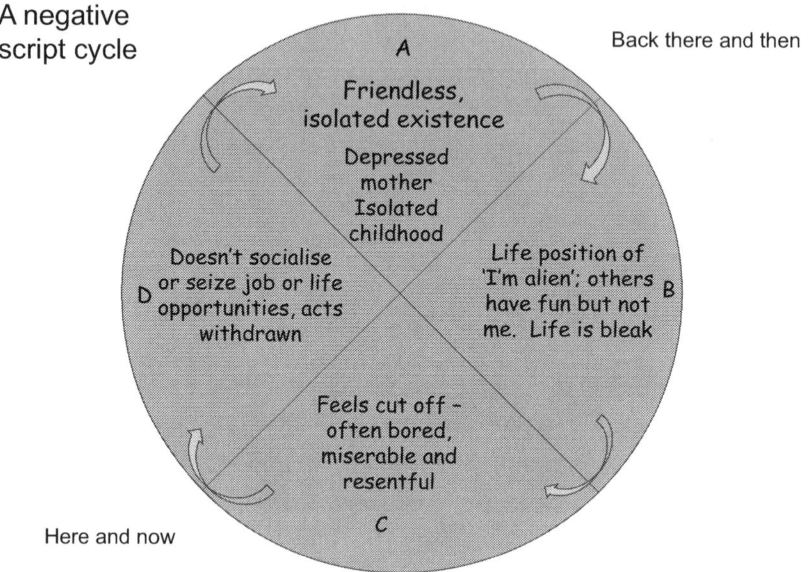

Figure 5.2 Colin's Script

mother was afraid that it was a rough neighbourhood. This, then, was his early protocol – being in a world that was bleak and empty, with a mother who was over-protective and at the same time unavailable.

Section B: internal structure: Colin's meaning-making, his script, both at the level of earliest non-conscious relational patterns and also at the level of conscious memory was that his sense of self-with-other was bleak and unnourishing, and that, while others seemed to enjoy life, it had little to offer him.

Sections C and D: here-and-now experience: At school, Colin had found it hard to make friends and did not join in activities like football or the school concert. It seemed that the teachers did not appear to notice his isolation. He was therefore co-creating repeats of his original experience of a bleak landscape where other people had fun but he did not. As an adult, he had a series of jobs, which he carried out competently. He was heterosexual and had had some girlfriends but none seemed to have become important. Colin's father had died some years before and he spoke of it without emotion. His mother had pre-senile dementia and was in long-term care. He had few friends and said that he spent most of his leisure time watching television or reading. As Colin told his story, he did so without much energy other than a slight sense of depressed resentment. When I asked him directly how he felt as he remembered the events he described, he sighed and said, 'Not great'.

From the start, I found Colin challenging to work with. We were very different personalities and at first I kept forgetting that empathic enquiries into his emotional state or what he might want would be met with, 'Fine' or 'What do you mean?' or, worse, a long intellectual description of himself as if he were a dissected frog (interestingly, his first job had been as a lab assistant, when dissections were his daily task). In addition, the stultifying early protocol had the effect of collapsing the space between us; the experience of vitality, of co-created relationship where novelty might occur, seemed impossible. We sat in a sort of mutual lifelessness and I struggled to stay engaged.

Things improved when I began to focus on Colin's behaviour and bodily sensations. In terms of the Script System, therefore, we started with identifying his behaviour, both in terms of his interactions with the world (largely dry and withdrawn) and also his 'micro-movements' in the sessions with me (Section D). Inviting him to connect with what he was experiencing (Section C) as he took the actions or non-actions he described, began to ignite an interest in and engagement with his own embodied self that was clearly new to him.

I introduced Colin to some of the models from transactional analysis (TA) and he was keen to build on that. (For readers unfamiliar with TA, two of the basic theories are briefly described in the boxes below.) To help him think about his behaviour at work, we talked about ego states and transactions, encouraging him to be more aware of different options as he related to people. As he began to connect with his immediate experience and the edges of his feelings and fears, suddenly the theories became full of meaning as he understood how the ulterior level of his communications conveyed the bleakness of his expectations. The impact was profound between us when one day he said that he could not attend the following session as he had 'a busy month at work'. I found myself agreeing to this without any reflection and only when I noticed his withdrawn expression did I realise that we had re-created an old dynamic. I had become the 'care-taking' figure who didn't care.

TA theory: ego states are the foundation concept of TA (Berne, 1961). The personality is understood to comprise a number of ego states that are formed as our script develops. They evolve over time as a result of our experiences in relationship to the environment. An ego state is a way of organising our experience as a set of feelings, thoughts and attitudes, sensations and behaviour (reminiscent of the core organisers – see Chapter 3).

Berne described three categories of ego state:

- *Parent* – sets of feelings, thoughts, attitudes and behaviour that are learned – often simply swallowed whole, as it were – from parent figures and other people who were significant and, to us, powerful as we were growing and developing our minds.

- *Child* – sets of feelings, thoughts, sensations, and so on, which are embodied experiences we had in childhood.
- *Adult* – sets of feelings, thoughts, sensations and behaviour which are influenced and affected by Parent and Child and are our way of meeting the world in the here and now. The Adult is sometimes referred to as the 'Integrating Adult' to represent its function of integrating these Parent and Child influences into our present-day functioning.

Ego states arise and recede in a dynamic way for us in different contexts. There is nothing intrinsically right or wrong with feelings, thoughts, experiences and behaviours associated with different ego states. Cultivating the present-moment awareness of the Adult supports us to notice what is arising and make choices about its appropriateness and usefulness in a particular context. This is especially true of the ego state modes – the behavioural model (see Figure 5.3). A client may be experiencing feelings and thoughts associated with Controlling Parent mode towards an underperforming employee and want to criticise, but an Adult may choose to bracket these feelings and impulses in order to support the employee's development with clear and detailed feedback, an interest in the employee's circumstances and offer of development. Another client, a leader working in a rather traditional organisation, may choose to bring their Child capacity for play, imagination and lightness into an innovation workshop requiring thinking outside of conventional parameters.

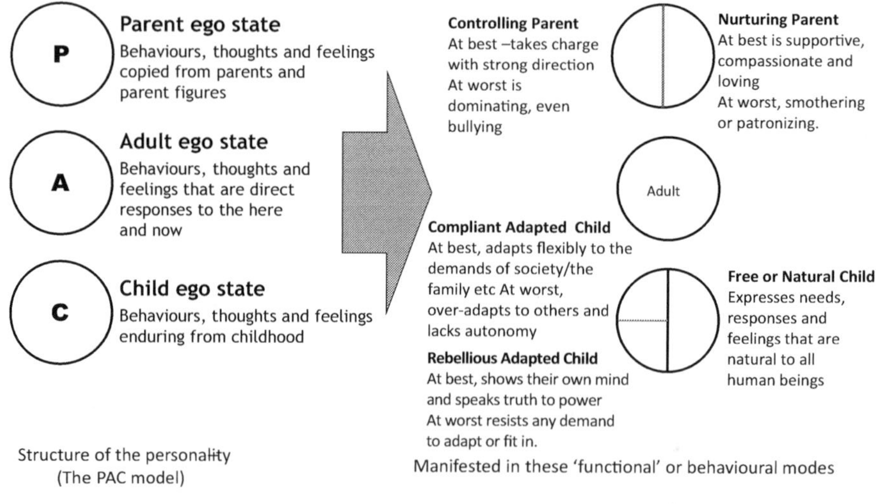

Figure 5.3 Ego states – the PAC Model (Berne, 1961) and Ego State Modes
Source: Adapted from Lapworth and Sills (2011)

TA Theory: Transactions are Eric Berne's theory of communication. There are three basic types of 'transaction' or relational exchange. Each is accompanied by a 'rule of communication'. See the diagrams below.

A *complementary transaction* is one in which the transactional vectors are parallel and the ego state addressed is the one that responds.

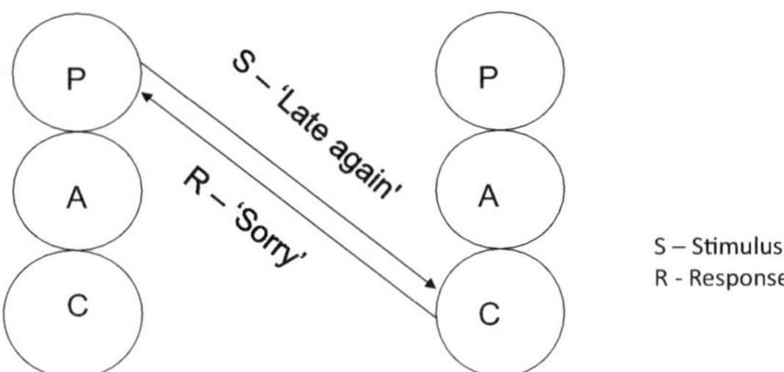

The rule is – so long as the transactions remain complementary, communication may continue indefinitely. (N.B. ComplEmentary means completing, compatible. Transactions are not necessarily complImentary!)

Figure 5.4 Complementary Transaction
Source: Adapted from Berne (1961, 1964)

A *crossed transaction* is one in which the transactional vectors are not parallel or in which the ego state addressed is not the one that responds.

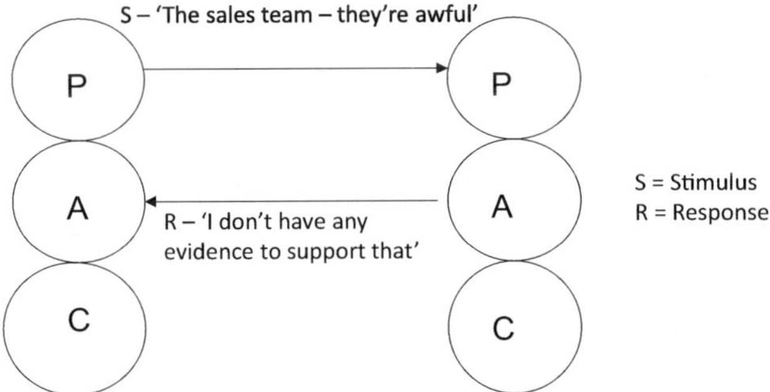

The rule is – when a transaction is crossed, a break in communication results and one or both individuals will need to shift ego-states in order for communication to be re-established.

Figure 5.5 Crossed Transaction
Source: Adapted from Berne (1961, 1964)

In an ulterior transaction, two messages are conveyed at the same time. One of these is an explicit or in Berne's terms 'social level' message (s), the other (illustrated by the dotted line) is an implicit or 'psychological level' message (p).

In Figure 5.6, both parties are aware that a 'secret message' was being exchanged. However, very often the ulterior message is largely or totally outside the person's awareness – it is the manifestation of a script adaptation that has become habitual (see Figure 5.7). We will explore this more in the following chapter.

In an *ulterior transaction*, two messages are conveyed at the same time. One of these is an explicit, overt or 'social level' message (s), the other (illustrated by the dotted line) is an implicit, covert or 'psychological level' message (p).

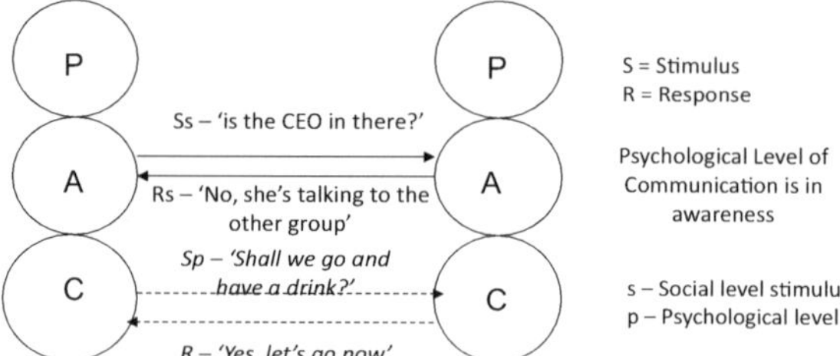

The rule is – the behavioural outcome of an ulterior transaction is determined at the psychological level and not the social level.

Figure 5.6 Ulterior Transaction
Source: Adapted from Berne (1961, 1964)

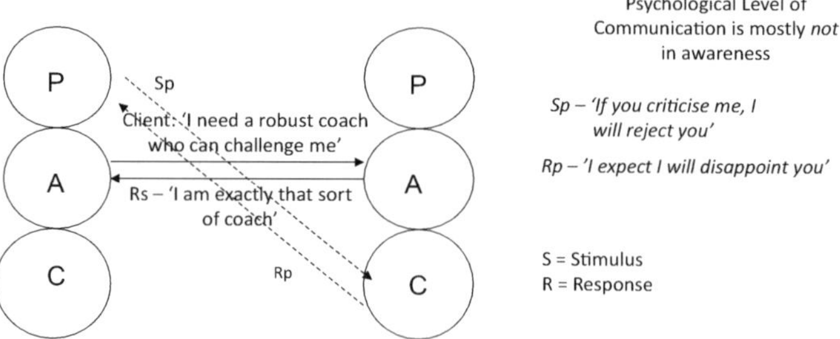

The rule is – the behavioural outcome of an ulterior transaction is determined at the psychological level and not the social level.

Figure 5.7 Ulterior Transaction: Psychological Level Out of Awareness
Source: Adapted from Berne (1961, 1964)

Colin experimented with acting differently in his relationships and was heartened by the results. He reported disagreeing with someone in a meeting and then offering his opinion in a straightforward (Adult ego state) manner. Others had shown interest and then asked him to give his views on something else. He had asked a colleague for help with a project and she had responded by suggesting they discuss it over a coffee. Colin looked positively excited as he told me about it.

Almost more important, however, was that connecting with his body sensations and feelings was linking to images, emotions and memories (link between Sections C and A – see Figure 5.2). Often, he noticed that if he followed his body he would discover tensions he did not know he had – impulses to push or to reach, impulses to yell. For example, as he acknowledged his feelings of anger at being overlooked for promotion, he was fascinated to feel the vitality of that experience, in contrast to how he 'depressed' the impulse to protest, lost energy and went passive.

There were times when Colin experienced me as not interested in him – projecting his mother onto me, if he thought I looked tired or distracted. This was the 'relational alchemy' that Ogden speaks of (Sensory Motor Institute). I listened carefully to him, sometimes I acknowledged the 'grain of truth' in his projections; sometimes I invited him to experience the fullness of his reactions. Occasionally, I gently pointed out that, in his mind, I had become one more person who was not taking care of him in the way that I should. Gradually, he began to allow himself to grieve, as he relived and talked about some of the lonely pain of his childhood. Letting go of that way of being, and risking wanting a different sort of life, required courage.

It also needed support. It was important that Colin restructure his life in order to provide more stimulation. In other words, while in the past his life had excessive amounts of predictability and structure, he had been very short of recognition, novelty and the opportunity to have an impact. Gradually, he began to change that. Although it still felt strange, he committed himself to joining some clubs, including a dating agency. He continued to meet his friendly colleague for social occasions and said it was the first time that he felt as if he was really getting to know a woman as a friend. Importantly, Colin was experiencing himself as more alive, he felt embodied in himself and (cautiously) revelled in experiencing his feelings and sensations. He also got a promotion.

USING THE SCRIPT CYCLE TO CHOOSE YOUR COACHING INTERVENTION

The strength of the script system model is that it offers a variety of ways of engaging with the client. It is possible to listen to the story of their life – either past or present (Section A) – and by raising awareness of the way they made sense of the world, the core beliefs they arrived at (Section B) and the emotional and somatic feelings that were either repressed or became habitual, patterns and beliefs become available for questioning and testing.

Alternatively, the relational coach can work exclusively in the present moment – with the client's accounts of his present-day experiences at work and with the potency of the here and now moment as past patterns are presented in the session with the coach (Sections C and D).

In particular, the relational coach will be interested in what relational 'third' occurs between them. What dynamics occur that might either reinforce old patterns (for both people) or offer an opportunity for a different experience? Neurobiological research (see, for example, Allen, 2000, for an accessible summary) has drawn the conclusion that real change can occur when in the presence of an empathic other, the pre-frontal cortex remains aware and functioning (i.e., in the present), while the body–mind is re-experiencing the past. In order to fully experience the past, the client will be in touch with their core organisers (see Chapter 3) as the coach invites them to mindfully explore them. This has the result of full self-awareness that allows the old material to be worked with (see also Beisser's paradoxical theory of change, 1970).

As can be seen in the example of Colin, it is important to work with the client in a way that is accessible. I (CS) suspect that Colin's encounter with therapy in the past was largely unsuccessful because he had firmly resisted the therapist's efforts to explore his feelings – not to be difficult, but because he was so disconnected from himself. They resorted to long discussions about his script beliefs and patterns that led nowhere. What brought some vibrancy and vitality to the coaching was the choice of keeping the focus on Colin's present behaviour and how he might change it. He began to have different experiences in his life as a result, which found a route through his dismissive style (*see* Attachment Styles below).

There is a link here to different 'channels of communication' – connection to self and to other. By 'channels' we mean that coach and client can make contact with each other through any of the core organisers – through thinking, through emotions, through embodied experience, through noticing their movement impulses and their sensations. It is useful for the coach to notice where their client is most accessible and to start with that channel, using it as a stepping stone to other less used channels. For example, one client might be very comfortable with and aware of their emotions. They meet the client telling their story with lots of emotional words and expressions of emotion. If the coach 'meets' them there, for example, by saying:

Coach: I hear how strongly you feel ...
Coach: How are you feeling as you say this to me?
Coach: You sound really sad/angry/anxious as you talk about that.

they can then be invited into other less aware channels – for example, thinking:

Coach: What do you believe about that?
Coach: What do you think that means?
Coach: What does that mean about you (or them or the organisation)?
Coach: I am curious about what lies behind your question to me.

Or into embodied experience:

Coach: What do you notice inside as you talk about that?
Coach: And your shoulders tense as you talk about that.
Coach: I notice that you smiled at that ... did you notice?

ATTACHMENT

Studies of attachment have revealed that the patterning or organisation of attachment relationships during infancy is associated with neuroplasticity, characteristic processes of emotional regulation, social relatedness, access to autobiographical memory, and the development of self-reflection and narrative (see, e.g., Main, 1995; Cozolino, 2016; Schore, 2016). All these capacities are crucial for leaders to be able to navigate the complexities of their roles, relationships and organisational contexts – themes that frequently arise in the context of a coaching engagement. Understanding attachment patterns can enable coaches and their clients to explore how the client's patterns might be shaping their responses to the situations they encounter.

Mary Ainsworth and colleagues (1978) devised an experiment to measure toddlers' responses to a strange situation. The researchers measured children's responses when their predictable structure and their attachment relationships were disturbed. They were interested in discovering the effect of this on children's capacity to explore the world and their way of relating to their caregiver.

They discovered that already at the age of two, infants seemed to have developed patterns in relation to their caregivers that affected and were affected by their developmental needs. They hypothesised a particular type of parenting that led to the development of these attachment styles. These styles seemed to stay with the individual, who would display a version of the same style as an adult. However, a child (and adult) might have a different style with, for example, one parent and another. For example, a little boy might ask his mother for a hug in a straightforward way, trusting that she will happily respond. The same child, however, may act quite formally and distant with their father, who, himself the product of a military family, sees vulnerability in a boy as a sign of weakness.

- A *secure attachment* style is characterised by making good contact with others, managing both separation and closeness appropriately and having the ability to reflect on the meaning of one's own and others' feelings, thoughts and behaviour.
- An *insecure avoidant* style tends to develop in a child whose parent(s) were themselves avoidant. Their emotional life was not attended to; there might even have been neglect. One way or another, the child decided that life

was less painful if they did not rely on support from outside, so they grew up avoiding closeness in relationship and, not infrequently, treating others rather dismissively.

- An *insecure ambivalent/anxious* style describes a person who is, in fact, preoccupied with others and what they think of them. They can be clingy and reluctant to find their independent voice.
- An *insecure disorganised* style is usually the result of a very disturbed early life where there might have been abuse, neglect or abandonment. Often the abuse came from the hands of the caretakers – in other words, the very person to whom one would turn for comfort was actually the source of the frightening or painful experience. An adult with a disorganised attachment style will be volatile and inconsistent – one moment phobic of being alone and the next pushing people away.

People are rarely uniformly in one style. They will, of course, shift as they are in relationship with others. For example, the most secure and relaxed of people can become avoidant when on the receiving end of the clingy advances of an ambivalent style. A relational coach will pay attention to their client's style and reflect on how they might be contributing to the response they are getting. Both coach and client will have their own attachment styles which can inform the relationship and how each experiences the other and thinks about the work as it unfolds.

Exercise 5.1

Reflection Alone

Identifying Your Own Attachment Style

Reflect on your own attachment style and the patterns of thinking, feeling and behaviour it gives rise to.

How do these patterns show up in your coaching practice – e.g., anxiety about being chosen for work; strong emotional reactions when not chosen; anxieties about giving the client what the client wants for fear of being rejected; difficulties with confronting interventions; ease and range across supportive and confronting interventions?

What support might you need to explore and expand your range beyond patterns associated with your attachment style if they are limiting you and your practice in some way?

How might you make use of your relationship with your supervisor to explore this?

What additional ongoing supportive strategies are available to you to support connecting with the capacities and perspectives of secure attachment?

CONCLUSION

There are myriad ways in which the client's – and the coach's – past emerges in the present.

We seem to cling to our script in ways that are hard to understand – even when we have begun to have insight about our patterns. We carry our attachment style into every relationship – sometimes a lot, sometimes a little. There are many reasons why old patterns are hard to budge – not only were they the ways that we learned early on that would at least in part get our needs met and secure the love we needed, but also they provide a sense of familiarity and certainty – a belief that we understand the world.

It is hoped that the here-and-now encounter with the coach in the session provides an opportunity to become aware of assumptions and habits, but also experience and experiment of new ways of being (see Chapter 7 on experiments in coaching) that might be more rewarding.

6

ENACTMENTS, GAMES, RUPTURES AND REPAIRS

In previous chapters we have emphasised the power of working in the present moment so that both client and coach have the experience of genuine meeting – having 'a conversation that they've never had before' (Richard Wainwright, personal communication). In Chapter 4, we offered a framework for the coach to listen to their embodied responses to their coaching client and to use those responses to further enquiry and meaning-making.

In this chapter, we explore ways of thinking and acting when the here-and-now relationship goes awry.

As we described in Chapter 5, our scripts can stay with us throughout our lives, shaping the way we meet the world (and ourselves). Sometimes the scripts of both client and coach find a hook in each other and they get into a relational pattern that risks reinforcing both their scripts. These relational patterns have a familiar feel to them because they are related to our scripts and they usually end up with us saying, 'How did I get here again?' There is wonderful learning in these moments, and it is important that the coach develops the skill of thinking about them with the client, without either party having to feel shame about getting into them.

In the world of psychotherapy and psychoanalysis, these interactions are often known as 'transferential enactments'. Taking a relational lens means moving away from the traditional ideas about transference and countertransference. In that old way of thinking, the client sees the coach as someone from their past and relates to them as if they were in fact that person, thereby inviting them into the transferential dance. The coach responds to that transferential gesture. This is called 'countertransference' or 'complementary countertransference' because the coach has begun to feel and act in the same way that someone in the client's past did. It is as if the coach is invited into a role in the client's script. Eric Berne, the founder of TA, developing the metaphor of the theatre, used to say that the client is like a casting director, looking around for people to cast as characters in their script.

Relational thinking recognises that we bring all of ourselves to every moment. In other words, even if someone invites us into a particular role or way of being, there must be something in us that gets hooked by the invitation. What happens between us is co-created. It is therefore more appropriate to think of *co-transference* in the enactment. In order to unpack the idea, we are again drawing on transactional analysis. Eric Berne was deeply committed to translating complex psychological concepts into accessible and practical ideas that will make sense to clients as well as practitioners. He called this type of relational interaction, in which the coach and client get entangled in something from their respective pasts, a 'game'. At first hearing, it seems a strange term for what is clearly an unhelpful, often distressing, script-reinforcing process. Indeed, Stuthridge (2015) called a game 'the intersection between two scripts'. However, Berne was attempting to point out that these repetitive patterns, like sports or board games that people play together, have rules of engagement, which have unconsciously become second nature. They follow clear steps, so that through an exchange of non-verbal interactions of which they are both unaware, the participants move inexorably to a predictable outcome. In that sense, they are like the rules of a regular game.

WHY PLAY GAMES?

There is much written about this topic in the TA literature. However, there are some basic elements to be found in all games:

- As games are part of our life script, then at some level they are all we know. We have no other way of being and behaving. Also, it can be disconcerting, even if ultimately less painful, to have our scripts challenged. Little (2006) points out that an old Parent–Child relational unit can be maintained as a defence against the loss of self and the loss of meaning.
- Games are attempts to get our needs met and negotiate the world within the limitations of our script. They are a source of 'strokes' – attention and recognition from another.
- In a strange way, they make life predictable. Human beings love certainty. It is not unusual to hear someone who has just realised they have been in a game say, 'I knew it... ' with some degree of satisfaction.

- Rather intriguingly, Berne implied that they fill time with familiar patterns and habits as a way of coping with the existential question of how to pass the time between birth and death.

WORKING WITH GAMES IN COACHING

In Chapter 5, we introduced the idea from transactional analysis of ego states comprising the Parent ego state – internalised experience of parents and significant others while growing up; the Child ego state – the thoughts, feelings, attitudes we experienced as children which were significant enough to shape our sense of self and the world; the Adult ego state – the experience of living in an aware 'present-centred' way. We described how communication could be understood as the relationship between these ego states and briefly outlined Berne's three types and rules of communication.

Games are 'sets of ulterior transactions, repetitive in nature, with a well-defined psychological payoff' (Berne, 1974, p. 23). In other words, they are an exchange of both explicit and implicit communications, the outcome of which is always determined at the ulterior or psychological (implicit) level. The 'payoff' is a familiar feeling that confirms the transference expectation.

In TA, it is common to think about *foresight, midsight* and *hindsight* in relation to games. Sometimes it is only when we experience the payoff that we are aware that we have played it (*hindsight*). This is because the implicit exchange is not in our awareness; it is a habitual part of our script. In this case, we can simply learn from the experience – how did we get triggered? What were we attempting to do with the other person? What were the ulterior messages that we were unconsciously sending and receiving? What part of our script might we be reinforcing? How might we do it differently in the future? In that way, we can strengthen our foresight.

Example

Jill came to supervision wanting to think about why she had a tendency to become confluent (over-identifying) with her clients, leading her to work hard to try to solve their problem and to take too much responsibility. She also realised that she wasn't challenging them. The supervisor enquired into the story. 'Was it all of her clients, or just some of them?' Jill was very clear that it was just some of them. As she explored, Jill realised what the clients had in common was that they were powerful women who were experiencing themselves as badly treated. Their colleagues and direct reports complained that they were angry and short-tempered with them, but they were surprised that nobody saw how vulnerable they were.

In an *ulterior transaction*, two messages are conveyed at the same time. One of these is an explicit or, in Berne's terms 'social level' message; the other (illustrated by the dotted line) is an implicit or 'psychological level' message.

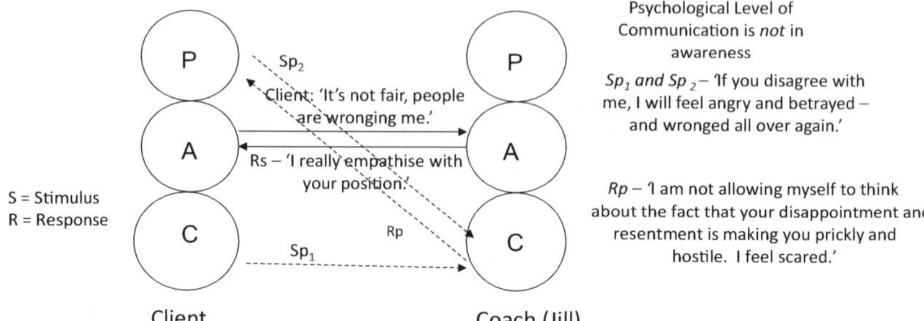

The rule is – the behavioural outcome of an ulterior transaction is determined at the psychological level and not the social level.

Figure 6.1 Ulterior Transaction: Psychological Level Out of Awareness
Source: Adapted from Berne (1961, 1964)

The reader will probably already have guessed that there was an echo of her relationship with her mother for Jill. Jill's role in the family was to be peacemaker. If she had tried to confront her mother in any way, there was likely to be punishment. Using the transactional diagram, Jill and her supervisor were able quickly to identify the transaction illustrated in Figure 6.1.

Remember that the ulterior level messages are genuinely largely unconscious. The client really does want to be recognised as the victim in the situation and the coach wants to be seen as a warm and supportive coach.

The payoff occurs when the ulterior levels of communication are enacted – for example, if the game had gone on unrecognised, Jill might eventually have invited the client to think about the impact she is having on her team. However, having delayed so long, her manner might have been abrasive. After coming to lean on the coach as being the supportive ally she had always wanted, the client might have felt shocked and betrayed, and quit coaching. Both coach and client would have reinforced their script beliefs: Jill that disagreement or confrontation would lead to punishment, and the client that everyone lets you down in the end.

In this case, Jill had had the *foresight* to bring the issue to supervision. Having identified the pattern and the 'script trigger', she could then prepare herself for future encounters that had a similar feel to them. She also realised that there was one particular client with whom she saw that she was deeply in the game. She considered her options and began to plan for how she might gently raise the topic in their next session. She had moved into *midsight*, which is when we become aware in the middle of a game that we are caught in something. We have a familiar emotion of anxiety, or we notice that we are working too hard, or behaving in some way that doesn't fit with our view of what a coach should be.

WHAT TO DO ABOUT GAMES

Jack Dusay (1966), a transactional analyst and colleague of Berne, claimed that there are four ways to address a game in midsight:

- Ignore the game
- Play the game
- Change the game
- 'Expose' the game

Ignore the Game

Here, the coach may recognise that a game is going on, but prioritise something else as more immediately important in service of the contract.

Example

Jim said, 'I don't know' when asked what he wanted to focus on and seemed to have forgotten their conversation of the previous week. His coach – Ellen – ended up guiding him and reminding him of what they had discussed. She planned to address this pattern but delayed doing so because of Jim's urgent need to consider his organisation's restructure and its impact on his team.

Play the Game

The coach suspects that they and their client are getting into a game, but is aware that they do not have much embodied response to what they have noticed. They judge that there is not enough evidence to make it worthwhile exploring. Instead, they wait for things to develop and become clearer.

Example

Ellen continues to take responsibility for reminding Jim what they have talked about. She even starts making notes after sessions and sending them to him, with a suggestion about what he could think about.

Change the Game

The coach crosses the transactions and shifts their own ego state to interrupt the ongoing exchange.

Example

Jim continues to be passive about his work and Ellen begins to notice her feelings of irritation. She realises that her responses are reminiscent of how she felt towards her younger brother, whom she took care of as a child. One day Jim asks his coach for her opinion: 'What would you do in my position?' Ellen replies with a smile: 'I wonder what you think I am going to say.'

Expose the Game

Here Dusay sounds as if he is being quite brutal and calling out the game in a 'j'accuse' sort of a way. However, if instead of the word 'expose' we think about collaboratively exploring what is happening in the relationship, this is the way that there can be rich learning for both people. The dynamic can be addressed in many ways.

- First the coach needs to draw attention to the pattern and invite the client to think about it: is it familiar? Have they also noticed it? How do they both feel? … and so on. Safran and Kraus (2014) call this 'meta-communication' – a communication about how we are relating.
- It is sometimes appropriate for the coach to 'go one down' at these times – for example, 'I notice that I keep making suggestions that you have already tried or are sure wouldn't work. I wonder what I am not hearing'. Or, 'I wonder how we get into this dance where I do … (description of behaviour) and you do …' Or, 'I might be completely missing the point but I wonder if …'
- If the coach wants to comment at the exact moment the behaviour is happening, it is important to be specific and in the present rather than comment on the trend – e.g., 'I notice that you are agreeing very fast with what I just said, as if you didn't need to think about it. What was happening for you just then?', rather than, 'I notice you have a tendency to agree very quickly with everything I say.' This type of comment risks pulling the client out of their lived experience into their head, to think about whether it is a pattern they know about themself. At worst, they may feel caught out and shamed.
- Ultimately, it might be appropriate to look at what underlying feeling is being avoided and what need both people are attempting to meet.

Example

Ellen started the session by asking Jim if he had thought about the note she had sent to him. Inevitably, Jim thanked her and said he had had a little time, but he had been very busy. Ellen said, 'Jim, have you noticed that we have got into an interesting pattern where you are so busy that you haven't time to concentrate on your development and so I jump in as your auxiliary brain and remind you what to think about?' Jim looked a bit uncomfortable and agreed, but said how useful the coaching was. Ellen said, 'How do you feel about that dynamic?' Jim looked baffled so Ellen went on, 'I am aware that I don't feel comfortable. I know that you are an extraordinarily bright man, but I end up treating you as if you can't think for yourself.'

Jim became very thoughtful and began to reflect on the impression he gave at the office by relying on others to remind him what was happening. Jim and Ellen returned to this topic several times in the coming sessions. Jim was increasingly insightful about his tendency to erase himself in situations where his Child ego state feared punishment. He made a link to 'keeping my head down' with his bullying father and how he constantly felt that he wasn't living up to what his father wanted. He was frustrated with himself and Ellen began to realise that his Parent ego state had become an inner critic to his shortcomings, joining Ellen in her irritation.

Ellen decided to offer what Martha Stark (2024) calls an 'optimally stressful' intervention, which names the stuck situation empathically, while leaving the dilemma with the client. She said, 'You know that you need to start making your own decisions and taking action, but at the moment it still feels too frightening to do that.' Jim teared up a little as he experienced Ellen's understanding and he softened towards himself.

Shortly after that, Jim reported taking more charge of his role at work. He also started journaling about his discoveries and thoughts.

Note: the 'optimally stressful intervention' names something that the client really does know but is stuck about, not one that the coach thinks he ought to know. Then it empathically meets the underlying feelings, making sure to say 'at the moment' or 'at present' to indicate that things can change.

THE DRAMA TRIANGLE

Another very useful model for understanding game dynamics is Stephen Karpman's (1968) 'Drama Triangle' (see Figure 6.2). Much has been written about this deceptively simple little model and if the reader is not familiar with it, there is a lot of helpful material online, including Steve Karpman's own website: www.karpmandramatriangle.com.

Basically, Karpman recognised that any game, regardless of the content and the people participating, involves three psychological roles – Victim, Rescuer and Persecutor. They are given capital letters in order to differentiate the psychological concept from real victims, rescuers and persecutors. When a person

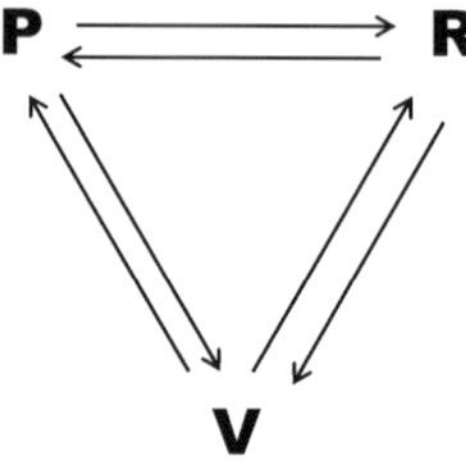

Figure 6.2 The Drama Triangle
Source: Karpman (1968)

is in one of these roles they are not using their full authentic self (including all their ego states) and/or not accounting for the other person's full authentic self. They are 'discounting' (Mellor and Schiff, 1975) some aspect of self, other and the situation.

Someone in the Victim position feels powerless and helpless and in need of another person to take charge of them. Someone in Rescuer believes that his or her mission is to take care of other people because other people can't take care of themselves. The person in Persecutor thinks that they should take charge and control those around him, as those people are inadquate and incompetent. The Persecutor is at best: dominating, and at worst: bullying. Persecutor is an extreme word, but the person in this role probably thinks that the world is in need of their guidance and ability to control. All three think that this is the only way that they will get their needs met (for love, for recognition, and so on). The game involves people moving through the positions on the triangle until the script reinforcing payoff is reached.

Thus, the drama triangle is a way that people negotiate power, responsibility and vulnerability between them. The positions we take will be deeply linked to our script.

The game starts when two people take up polarised positions on the triangle – positions that resonate with their scripts. Often the third position is avoided. In the example above, Jim was in Victim and Ellen was in Rescuer. Occasionally, they swapped roles when Jim reassured Ellen that her coaching was useful.

Had they not collaborated to explore the pattern, they might have played it through to the end. This is likely to have been one of three outcomes: Ellen might have taken the Persecutor position and become critical, nagging or dismissive. Or Jim might have been sacked for failing to deal with redundancies in his team effectively (here the Persecutor role is 'out-sourced' to the organisation), leaving Ellen feeling like the inadequate, guilty Victim for not having helped Jim. Or Jim might have told Ellen that the coaching had not been helpful after all (he would probably say, 'You didn't challenge me enough') and Ellen would end up in Victim. Meanwhile, Jim, briefly in Persecutor, slides back into Victim.

One could imagine the script-forming situations that might lie behind each of these outcomes, and sometimes it is appropriate to do that sort of trace-back to the origins of patterns. However, the beauty of Karpman's drama triangle is that it is not necessary to go back and explore the story behind a person's patterns. It can be enough simply to recognise our tendencies and become skilled at noticing the dynamics as they unfold in the moment. The embodied self-awareness described in Chapter 4 can be helpful here.

Acey Choy (1990) wrote an article called 'The Winner's Triangle' in which those three psychological roles are distortions of positive intentions. Choy describes them as Assertive, Caring and Vulnerable, and identifies certain skills associated with each position that can turn it from a game role to a quality (1990, p. 42). She says that in each position self-awareness is important and the willingness to use all of ourselves. The Persecutor needs to learn assertiveness in order to act in his own interest, not dominate others. The Victim needs to learn to think for themself and problem solve. And the Rescuer – the position most favoured by coaches – needs to learn and listen.

Locate the Client's Issue with the Client

The drama triangle illustrates very well how game roles are two sides of a conflicting issue. They often represent the client's inner conflict or inner dialogue. The goal is for the coach to help the client own both sides of a game. Stuthridge (2015) and Stuthridge and Sills (2019) argue that the coach needs to 'go first' in this and recognise both roles in their own self first. If they own their roles, it is more likely that their client will be able to as well.

In the example of Ellen and Jim above, Ellen had to own her own feelings of helplessness and self-doubt in the face of her failure to help Jim change, feelings that lay underneath the irritation. When she had done that, she could make the invitation that would allow Jim to do the same.

Look to the Contract

Margaret Turpin, a senior figure in the TA world, used to say (personal communication, sometime in the 1980s): 'If you have a game you don't have a contract, if you have a contract, you (probably) won't have a game.'

If in a session, the coach, with midsight, realises that a familiar dynamic is emerging – or even an unfamiliar one but one that doesn't feel right – it is often helpful to make an in-the-moment contract. For example, 'What would you like from me about this?' or 'Is this useful right now?', and so on. Re-establishing agreement about goals, tasks and bonds (Bordin, 1979; see Chapter 2) can get the work back on track.

RUPTURE AND REPAIR

Jeremy Safran talks about 'alliance ruptures': breakdowns in communication and rapport between coach and client. (Safran is actually talking about therapists, but as we have already discussed in Chapter 2, the coaching research supports the findings of psychotherapy outcome research in emphasising the importance of the working alliance, whatever the theoretical approach of the coach.)

Alliance ruptures can range from a brief moment of misattunement, such as an inadvertent crossed transaction (see Chapter 5) that is quickly recovered, through to a serious rupture in the rapport and empathic bond in the relationship, which at worst leads to the breakdown and cancellation of the coaching. Safran acknowledges that a rupture can be the result of an enactment of the two people's script patterns – what we are calling here 'a game' – but his concept is not confined to that. He believes that a rupture in the alliance occurs 'every session or two'. He argues that any intervention by a coach – or indeed by a client – needs to be understood in the context of its relational meaning. The same comment or question might land very well with one client but be experienced as critical, intrusive or patronising by another, depending on who they are, the nature of their script, the previous conversations between coach and client, the tone of voice and micro gestures of the coach's delivery, and so on.

Safran thinks that alliance ruptures are often characterised by tensions around goals and tasks. He believes that those apparently simple negotiations about where the coaching is headed and how the participants will work together can be the context in which the dialectic between autonomy and agency on one hand and the drive for relatedness on the other, emerges. In other words, coach and client have different minds and different views about meanings, what is useful, and so on. In addition, there will be many other differences between them, such as gender, age, race, sector experience, class, sexuality, and so on. This is one of the reasons we think that a conversation in which coach and client share their intersectional identity is so important. The client (or indeed the coach) needs to have permission to name it if they think wrong assumptions are being made or some aspect of their identity is misunderstood or ignored. These small collisions of difference are balanced against the desire on both sides for connection, meeting and rapport. In truth 'true autonomy (…) can only be achieved in the context of true relatedness' (Safran, 2003, p. 458) and vice versa.

Further, the process of negotiating ruptures followed by repair is a crucial developmental achievement and ongoing challenge. Safran's research shows that if they are a part of a person's therapeutic (and coaching) journey, that is an indicator of positive outcome (Safran et al., 2011). It follows, therefore, that it is important for the coach to look out for signs of a rupture in the contact and pay attention to it. Otherwise, true authentic meeting cannot take place.

Safran stresses that coaches should always pay attention to the impact they are having on their client. He identifies two signs that there has been a rupture. The first is withdrawal on the part of the client who might avert his gaze, go silent or simply comply with the coach's suggestions. The coach can use any of the interventions described above and in previous chapters to work in the moment with this. They might say, 'What happened then? It looks as if my last remark didn't land well,' or 'I think I may have been clumsy then,' or 'You may not agree with what I said – I hope you will tell me,' and so on. If the coach gently explores, it may emerge that the client was feeling criticised or missed in an important way. If they can together stay with the tension and uncover how the client feels and what he needs, they can move to a position where they can both be, in Winnicott's (1971) words, 'good enough'.

The second sign of a rupture will be open confrontation, disagreement or anger. This one is easier to spot, of course, but it is tempting for coaches to get defensive or start explaining themselves. Instead, staying empathic and recognising the impact of what they have said and done can also help the client express their hurt feelings and their need for support.

CONCLUSION

In the course of relational coaching, it is inevitable that there will be times when the strong bond between coach and client will be interrupted or when old relational dynamics start to take over the immediacy of the encounter. These moments should not be a cause of shame or embarrassment for either party. On the contrary, they should be welcomed as often the only way that deep, unaware processes can be surfaced and understood. Frequently, these processes are implicated in the client's presenting issues and challenges and, if sensitively attended to, provide the opportunity for something new and creative to emerge. The client and coach can now develop more flexible ways of relating, which can result in new perspectives, choices and action in clients.

In the next chapter, we explore ways that the coach can use the here-and-now relationship for experimenting with new ways of being in the world.

7

EXPERIMENT AND CHANGE

Experiments are specific interventions designed to raise the client's awareness in relation to their issues. They invite them to 'try on' different ways of being and behaving. We are drawing on the centrality of awareness in Gestalt psychology (Perls, 1969/1992) as a force for supporting change to occur in clients, be this changes in awareness, insight, perspective, range of choice, skill and options for action. In Chapter 4, we explored in detail how the coach can become present to their own experience, attune to the client, notice what resonates in their own body and then articulate invitations informed by this experience. Experiments are a particular form of articulation and need to be informed by the relational dynamics of the coaching relationship. They are not predetermined exercises, protocols or techniques imposed upon the client irrespective of what is happening moment by moment.

Experiments are very much a practice of the Gestalt tradition (see, for example, Zinker, 1977; Perls et al., 1951/1989; Joyce and Sills, 2018). They are active interventions informed by what resonates with the coach in relation to the client, and what each is experiencing in the co-created dynamic of the coaching conversation and the focus of the work. Experiments are intended to move from talking about something to experiencing something directly, by doing something different, moving differently, or imagining and exploring either a challenging or a desired situation. They can be used to expand awareness. They can also be used to see what happens if a familiar pattern of thinking/behaving is interrupted to make room for new possibilities.

Experiments are based on paying careful attention to what is experienced in the here and now and on discovery through doing. In experiments the quality of the coach's and client's ability to connect with experience, and their awareness of sensory, emotional and mental processes that arise, is key. As we set out in Chapters 3 and 4, making use of the core organisers of the present moment when experimenting with clients will support awareness as well as the discovery of new perspectives and implications for taking different action. It is not possible to predetermine what will happen in an experiment and the focus remains on increasing awareness of what emerges as the experiment unfolds. Facilitating clients to have a more direct experience that allows them to embody and connect with it more deeply, express an emotion or enact a behaviour, can be a powerful catalyst for change.

THE SEQUENCE OF AN EXPERIMENT

Experiments can be broken down into a series of overlapping stages. These can occur in any order but commonly follow the same sequence.

1. Identifying the Emerging Focus of the Work

In Gestalt, this focus is referred to as the figure (Perls, 1969/1992) – that which comes into focus and captures the attention of coach and/or client. It is what begins to resonate for coach and/or client (as we described in Chapter 4).

2. Suggesting an Experiment

This is where the coach builds on what is resonating and offers to the client the possibility of an experiment. Articulation and the suggestion of an experiment needs to be offered with a lightness of touch to gauge the client's levels of interest and willingness to try it. Equally, as the client becomes familiar with the immediacy of this way of working, they might also suggest an experiment. For example, the client might say, 'I notice my legs are beginning to tighten and push against the floor, as though they want to get up and move. I will see what happens when I do.' When working with the wisdom of the body (and in particular if the work is online so the coach's view of the client's body is limited), it is especially important to engage the client's collaboration as they will be in a strong position to notice their own bodily experiences.

3. Grading the Experiment for 'Risk' and Challenge, and Developing the Experiment

Grading the Level of Challenge

Change happens when we encounter a novel experience – something that takes us out of our familiar range and repertoire of thoughts, feelings and behaviours. This is how change emerges from the interaction of coach and client as each enter into a free-flowing process in which their individual experiences, feelings and thoughts act as sources of difference and novelty. Moving beyond what is habitual or familiar can be exciting but also cause anxiety.

Fritz Perls famously described fear and anxiety as unsupported excitement (1969/1992). Here he is pointing to the need to pay attention to the client's levels of psychological support when experimenting with new possibilities and experiences. The degree of exposure that the experiment represents needs to be carefully explored and negotiated between coach and client.

For example, a client may be feeling so angry with a colleague that they cannot think clearly about what options they have for confronting the colleague. They may be fearful of their anger taking over and saying or doing something they may later regret. The coach might gently suggest that the client express their anger directly in the coaching session, where they would be safe to speak uncensored, with no consequences. The client may recoil from this idea, fearing judgement from the coach or being overcome by anger. The coach might offer some support in the form of reminding the client of the confidentiality agreement they both have and that there are no consequences of saying what the client really feels as nobody but the coach is in the room. If the client still finds it difficult to say anything, the coach might experiment with different grades of experiment such as:

- Inviting the client to notice the feeling of anger and allow it to sit in their body, even if they cannot give words to it.
- Exploring with the client what beliefs and assumptions they have about anger. (Anger in its pure form is information that someone – or life – is doing something that is hurtful to us. But it's an emotion that gets bad press as it can be used to hurt people.)
- Exploring on a scale of 1–10 how able the client feels to confront their colleague.
- Exploring the mildest form of confrontation the client feels is possible for them and then gently inviting the client to explore what turning up the intensity and directness of the confrontation in tiny increments might be like.

Throughout this process, the coach can make use of the core organisers to explore how the client is experiencing the grading and notice any new discoveries that might be revealing themselves.

Developing the Experiment

There are many ways in which coach and client can deepen and develop the experiment. We list some of them below, but encourage the reader to be co-creative with their client – remembering that it is not about resolving a problem or finding a solution. It is about playing with or 'trying on' expanding possibilities.

- Staying with and exploring the here-and-now thoughts, feelings and sensations (as described in Chapter 4).
- Amplification or moderation of movement, sensation, gestures. The coach might say, 'How about saying that again only more loudly?' Or 'Make that gesture a bit bigger – how does that feel?' Or alternatively, 'Slow down a little, really stay with that tiny movement and what it wants to do … don't act on it yet … stay with the impulse.'
- Directing awareness. For example, 'And what is happening in your arms (or legs, or body or neck, etc.) as you say that?' Or 'Is there an emotion that goes with that?'
- Guided visualisation. For example, 'So with this new-found confidence, imagine yourself walking into the office tomorrow morning. What will be different? How will you look? What will you do?', and so on.
- Using creative media – drawing, painting, collage, plasticine/clay – to represent a not-yet-fully-formed experience, or to engage more right hemispheric processing into a cognitive narrative.
- Using other forms of expression – music, singing, poetry, etc.
- Exploring the polarity (opposite) of familiar and current experience. Zinker (1977) suggests starting by exaggerating the current state and discovering whether the polarity emerges. But the coach can also invite the client to 'walk the continuum line' between the present and its opposite, exploring how the client would be at every stage. Or they could introduce the client to the idea that their preferred quality or way of being might be the other side of a disliked, disowned or undeveloped quality. For example, a client's Driver behaviour (see Chapter 3) is part of the meaning-making part – Section B – of their script system (see Chapter 5). Their belief might be 'I am only OK if I am … e.g., very strong or take care of everyone, or please everyone'. Any glimmer of the opposite quality is a 'script backlash' and deeply unsettling to them. Raising awareness of that might allow a client to experiment with owning the disowned part with perhaps empty chair or ego state dialogue (see following point).

- Empty chair work – putting different aspects of the client or the client's experience on different chairs; the client then moves between chairs and dialogues with different parts, all the while paying attention to their experience. In TA, this would be an ego state dialogue and this can be useful short-hand if the client is familiar with those ideas.
- Empty chair work to explore a relationship with a colleague or manager – to uncover the client's real feelings about them. Also, if appropriate, to have the client try on the colleague's shoes, as it were, and imagine how they may be feeling. This exercise can be used with figures (e.g., Lego) or objects to represent the participants, but if it is possible to actually move to another chair, it is remarkable how the client often finds a level of understanding that they did not have before.
- Building somatic resources (Ogden et al., 2006). Careful tracking of the core organisers can lead to recognition that the client is unsupported or unresourced in some way. The coach can design an experience to support them – in breathing, for example (deep silent breathing in and out for a count of 5 or 6 seconds), or grounding (connecting with the earth through the soles of the feet or the weight of the body in the chair), or containment (feeling the boundaries of the body) or alignment of the spine and neck to increase strength and confidence.
- Completing 'unfinished business'. This concept – again from Gestalt – includes undoing the retroflection of repressed feelings (the tendency to turn repressed feelings inwards – for example, being angry at oneself instead of towards a colleague). It allows a person to give voice to unacknowledged experiences. It can also mean completing the 'interrupted gesture'. For example, a client becomes aware that as they talk about their bullying boss, they are slightly leaning away from the memory and image of their angry shouting. In the session, the client allows themself not only to lean, but to stand up and move away out of range. They also experiment with saying out loud, 'I'll talk to you later when you are less upset.' They then start to laugh at the idea of saying this to their boss. They later report feeling much less trapped.
- Stakeholder mapping – using Post-it Notes or objects on the desk to represent people, market trends or parts of the organisation, recognising who/what is relevant and what connections there are between them. The client can experiment with moving the people around, as in a constellation or sculpt. See how the closeness or distance makes a difference.

During this process, the coach stays alert to signs that the client might be getting triggered by the challenges of the exercise. The aim is to stretch the edges of the client's window of tolerance (see Chapter 3) in order to create what Perls et al. (1951/1989, p. 288) called the 'safe emergency' without the client becoming dysregulated. There are different ways of regulating the levels of risk, anxiety and exposure as an experiment progresses:

- Ask the client to stop for a moment and breathe or feel their feet on the floor.
- Suggest that the client pause and take stock of their experience.
- Remind the client that you are there as support.
- Suggest that the client stands up to feel more grounded and resourced in their body.
- Change the situation – e.g., you might say, 'I want you to imagine that your manager cannot speak for the moment and they just listen to what you have to say.'
- Suggest that the client imagines someone to support them that they can take with them in their mind's eye when they are facing a challenging situation. The coach might say, 'Do you know anyone who you think would manage this situation well … either a real person or a character from a book or film? Imagine them standing beside you …', and so on.
- Building a somatic resource (see above).

4. Completing the Work

The same client who feels they need to confront their colleague may discover what they want to say to their colleague and how they want to say it. They may experience some clarity and excitement at the possibility of breaking a familiar pattern of accommodating others and not asserting themself. They may say they feel more solid and strong, like a mountain.

5. Assimilating and Integrating the Learning

Here the coach acknowledges what the client has achieved and slows the client down so they can really experience the shifts that have occurred in energy, confidence and clarity. Using the map of the core organisers, the coach might ask the client to feel into their new-found clarity and confidence. The coach might say, 'I notice that as you said you see a way forward, your shoulders went down and your back straightened … do you notice that? What else do you notice?' They can gently direct the client to feel into sensations, emotions and movement impulses that may arise. The coach may invite the client, if they are willing, to imagine the conversation, seeing their colleague in their mind's eye and checking in with their sensations, emotions, movement impulses, thoughts. If at any point the client begins to feel anxious, the coach might, again gently, remind them to sense more into the feeling of confidence and solidity, reconnecting with the image of a mountain that they experienced earlier to remind the client that they can manage their own state in the face of a challenging situation. As the client connects more with the sensations of strength and feeling clearer about what they want to say, the coach may invite the client to imagine taking this feeling of substance, solidity and clarity into their meeting with their colleague.

CONCLUSION

Most of this book emphasises the importance in relational coaching of recognising and staying with 'what is' in the present moment. Following Beisser's paradoxical theory of change (described on p. 35), we strive to amplify a client's (and coach's) experience and awareness of who they are and what might be happening between them. The coach trusts that through collaborative enquiry, something new will emerge.

In this chapter, however, we have been introducing a very different approach – one that, while staying true to the emergent, invites play, experimentation, trying on the new, with a view to an expansion of possibilities and of world view. It is a way of playing with present experience *in* the present, in order to change the past. In other words, it offers the possibility of creating new meaning-making and a loosening of script.

ENDINGS IN COACHING

Our working lives are full of endings and transitions, perhaps especially these days as businesses strive to respond to a rapidly changing world. Not only do restructuring, staff changes and team fluidity create transitions that must be managed, but also the days of staying in a company for life seem to have gone forever. According to Janet Sheath (personal communication), who directs the Career Coaching programme at Birkbeck University, these days someone may expect to have many different careers in their working lifetime.

THE IMPORTANCE OF ENDINGS

Every change, every new start, involves an ending – a period of transition from ending the old and adjusting to the new. We develop our individual patterns of managing them – some useful and some less so. Often, coaching will have included helping clients to adjust well to change – in role, in organisation, in life circumstance. Part of a coach's job is to help the client become aware of their own pattern in relation to endings and change. That way, the client can support themselves when beginning new relationships, transitioning between relationships and through all types of endings, all of which are a common feature of matrix organisations.

Example

I (CS) worked with John who came to coaching because he was feeling very anxious in his new role. He had been country manager in his company and although English himself, had been living for several years in Japan, married to a Japanese woman. Recently, they had relocated to South London and he had taken the job of European regional manager.

John was worried that the role demands were more than he could meet. He was sleeping badly and having panic attacks. When I enquired carefully, it seemed to me that his very successful career suggested that he would be well able to fill the role. I was baffled at his lack of confidence. Something made me explore his history in relation to job changes and transitions in general. John told me – without seeming to make the connection – that he had a similar period of anxiety and depression when he first moved to Japan and before that, when he took his first job abroad in (then) Yugoslavia. He was intrigued when I suggested that his current anxiety might be related to his difficulty adjusting to change.

Further enquiry revealed that John's childhood was filled with painful leavings, which included leaving the family home when his parents divorced and going to boarding school at the age of nine. With some relief at the dawning awareness, as well as grief at the memories, John began to make sense of what was happening to him.

THE END OF THE COACHING ENGAGEMENT

Sometimes, it is only towards the end of the coaching engagement that the opportunity emerges to work with endings. This can be transformative for the client and, indeed, the coach.

Why do we think that working with endings is so important, even for people who have not suffered such grievous losses as John had? The answer to that question is both simple and profound. Endings, separations, losses and transitions shape the way we are and how we act in the world – including how we relate to others – perhaps more than any other life experience. We have already looked at the impact that early childhood can have on a script – our way of being in the world. It is in those early years that the infant and young child are exposed to many changes and separations, and their experience of those will be key to the stability of their sense of self in relationship. A baby starts life in the womb, conceived in relationship, inseparable from its mother. From the moment of birth they have to gradually adjust to being separate individuals. Infant research shows very clearly that babies have 'conversations' with their mothers – making vocal calls, facial expressions and body movements in ways that show a sense of self/other long before there is a sense of ego self. The so-called 'still face experiment' is distressing to watch (search 'Still Face Experiment', e.g., on YouTube). It shows the swift response of panic, agitation and grief when a baby's mother (instructed by the researchers) for a minute stops responding lovingly to the infant and turns her face blank. Clearly, the attachment to the mother is all-important. It is distressing precisely because somewhere we can all resonate with that little person's sense of baffled abandonment. Fortunately, the abandonment is quickly repaired as the mother turns back and resumes the loving interchange.

At this age, the infant's experience is very much a series of bodily-affective states. If the interaction with the environment – usually in the person of mother – is 'good-enough', as Donald Winnicott (1965) famously said, it provides an experience of soothing and regulating, which is the stimulus for laying down the neural pathways in the brain of the largely undeveloped cortex. This is the beginning of consciousness and the capacity of the baby to 'hold' itself and regulate itself. The beginning of the sense of self.

With this sense of self comes a sense of other. The child's experience of self with other will be the early map of the attachment pattern and, very likely, the core of the script (see Chapter 5). There follows a series of ordinary losses and necessary adjustments, such as the realisation that other people are important to mother in addition to them having to make space for siblings, going to school, not winning the prize, moving house, and so many more. There might also be less 'ordinary' losses – such as the death of a family member, becoming ill, parental separation – that will contribute to the tapestry of meaning-making that is the development of script.

These early relational experiences make us sensitive to connection and disconnection throughout life and lead us to develop an attachment style that will colour future relationships. In Chapter 5, we described the four attachment styles that were identified by theorists such as Main (1995) and Ainsworth et al. (1978) – one secure and three so-called 'insecure' styles: avoidant, anxious/ambivalent and disorganised (see Figure 8.1). They are very relevant when thinking about endings, change and transition because they were originally developed by watching the reaction of young children to temporary separation from their mothers. We recapitulate the description of them here with a focus on their response to endings.

The Attachment Styles

Secure Style

The individual with a secure attachment style:

- Will seek appropriate support and work through the tasks of ending.
- Can feel a range of feelings about the ending, including anger, sadness, appreciation.
- Can articulate a narrative about their relationship with the lost 'object' (role, organisation, colleague, status, and so on).

- Can articulate both positive and negative thoughts and feelings about the situation.
- Can plan for the future appropriately.
- Can go on thinking in the face of uncertainty, ambiguity and 'not knowing'.

Insecure Preoccupied (Or Anxious/Ambivalent)

The individual with an insecure preoccupied (ambivalent) style:

- Will be emotional and clingy, very distressed at a loss or major change.
- Can often need a lot of support, including from the coach.
- Can resist attempts to get them to think and plan their life.
- Can be over-adapting or agitating.
- Can have many unresolved issues, expressed through narratives of not feeling complete.

Insecure Dismissive (Or Avoidant)

The individual with an insecure avoidant (dismissive) style:

- May feel depression or have somatic symptoms.
- May feel very resistant to receiving help.
- May have no real coherent narrative about their relationship with the past or whatever is ending.
- May react to even small changes by withdrawing – for example, after a break in the work where the coach may be away, might miss a session or go through the PA to rearrange.
- May minimise the significance of the change or ending.

Insecure Disorganised

The individual with an insecure disorganised style:

- Will have no articulate narrative.
- Will have few positive feelings about a lost object, yet the loss is of immense importance.
- Can be either very fearful or very controlling.
- Where they lose a person or job they cared for, it can trigger 'compensated' pathology – e.g., dissociative disorder.
- May be vulnerable and at risk.
- Is unlikely to seek coaching, but if they do, it is likely that the coach can be most useful in supporting them to move into psychotherapy.

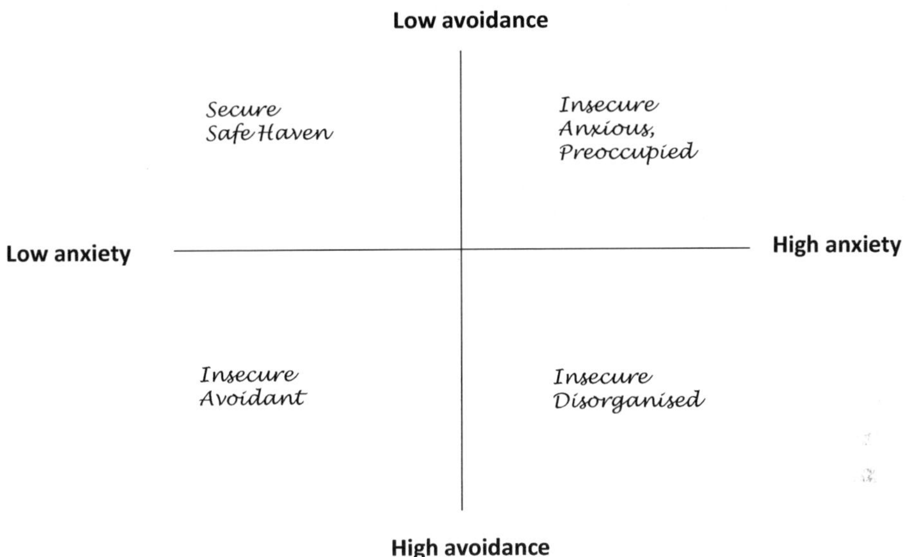

Figure 8.1 Attachment Patterns
Source: Adapted from Ainsworth and Bell (1970); Main et al. (1965); Bowlby (1969, 1973)

It can be useful to hold the framework in mind when helping people think about their patterns around endings. Also, there is no doubt that if we, as coaches, can model being regulated, contactful and able to stay in touch with ourselves and others, this will contribute hugely to the client's ability to do the same.

You, reader, at this point, may well be thinking that we are making a lot of this. We are talking about a client's ordinary working life with its ordinary, everyday changes and transitions. And, of course, you would be right. Many of our clients will adapt to change easily and flexibly. However, we believe that many of us struggle subtly, not even acknowledging that struggle to ourselves. We have found that having a perspective on attachment and its relationship to managing transitions and challenging situations can be a useful map for helping clients understand their struggles and patterns. It enables coaches to normalise these very human experiences and explore how coaching clients might support themselves at times of change with the inevitable disorientation that can come with them. It is rarely unhelpful to raise someone's awareness of how they manage change, and the ending of coaching is a great opportunity. Sometimes it is absolutely vital to a client's well-being, as in the case of John. We will return to him later in the chapter.

COMMON PATTERNS OF ENDING

There are, of course, as many patterns around endings as there are unique individuals. However, broadly there are five common responses.

Denying the ending – 'This is not really a goodbye. Our paths will cross many times in the future.' 'The group will get together next year at… .' 'We have each other's Whatsapp addresses so we can keep in touch.' 'Can we get together for lunch from time to time?', and so on.

Hanging on – Often revealed by comments like, 'I don't feel that I have learned nearly enough. Can we set up another set of six sessions?'

Leaving early – Sometimes clients 'refuse' to have their last session in order not to face the finality of an ending. This might be physical, as in, 'I am sorry but an important meeting has gone into my diary. I will have to miss my last session.' Alternatively, the early leaving might be psychological, 'I am excited about the new job/holiday/stage of my development that is starting on Saturday.' It can be useful to ask them to notice if they have lots of 'not quite finished' situations that add to their experience of being overwhelmed by the demands of work.

Idolising the coach – 'This has been absolutely marvellous!' 'You are a superhero!' and so on, which denies the real feelings about the real experience of parting.

Denigrating/discounting the relationship – For example, 'There wasn't enough … .' 'It was nice to have someone to talk to, but I think I was making those changes anyway.'

Do you notice any echoes of your own patterns? What might be the coach's version of hanging on, of leaving early, of denying, and so on?

The Tasks of the Coach

There are no particular skills involved in working with endings in coaching that are different from skills relating to coaching in general. The one important skill, if one can call it that, is to recognise endings and their significance, to be ready to talk about endings and explore their meaning for the client. That means that the coach must have done their own inner work and be familiar with their own patterns around endings. If we do not do that, we will likely impose our own patterns on our clients and at the very least deprive them of their own experience.

If you have not already worked on your own patterns, we invite you to do the exercises below as an enquiry. They might also be relevant to do with your clients if together you begin to realise that transitions are particularly difficult for them.

Exercise 8.1

On Your Own or with Your Client

Tracking Life Changes

Draw a line across a page to represent your life, from conception to the present day.

Mark off (roughly) the decades and then mark, like the measurements on a ruler, the major changes you experienced and the age you were when they happened. Allow your heart to lead you in this. In other words, if something felt like a significant change, put it on the time line. It can be a tiny loss or a big one. Don't start judging its magnitude objectively or comparing yourself to a starving child who loses their home.

For every event pause, enquire into your experience using the core organisers (see Chapter 3).

Ask yourself, 'How did I survive/manage that change or loss? What helped? Who else was there? Was I supported? Was I given space to say what was going on for me?' Do you notice any repeating pattern about how you coped with change?

Exercise 8.2

On Your Own or with a Partner

First Day at School

Recall your first day at school. You are unlikely to be able to remember a lot of detail. When we go through major changes like this, it is akin to being thrown, without much preparation or local knowledge, from a small family-run organisation into a huge, anonymous conglomerate. We don't organise our thoughts very well and often don't lay down narrative memories, as in trauma.

If you grew up in the UK, you will have started school at age four or five. You might have started at nursery even earlier than that. If you were fortunate enough to be brought up in a country where you did not start school until you were older, there may have been other major transitions, losses or changes previously. You may choose to use one of those for this exercise.

Allow yourself to recall whatever you can. What can you remember feeling? What happened? And then what did you feel?

See if you can synthesise the story down to its bare bones.

Examples

(These are all true stories with names and details changed. All of them are about boys, with different experiences.)

Deepak went to the school where his older brother was already established. His brother took him into the school and helped him settle in. They played together at break time and Deepak proudly introduced him to his new friends.

Joe's mother dropped him at school and left him in the playground – urging him to go and play with the other boys. Joe felt scared but didn't say so because he knew that his mother was upset and harassed.

Bob cried and pulled at his mother's hand, but she left him anyway.

Jason was furious – raged at his mother and the teacher and then jumped out of the window to run away. He broke his leg and subsequently got lots of attention from classmates who were impressed at his bold gesture and queued up to sign his plaster.

Next, does the story hold the seed of how you might manage endings? You might want to do this with a partner who will help you find the thread.

Examples

Deepak approaches new beginnings with positivity. He tends to look for an 'older' colleague to befriend and mentor him, and he expects to get on well with his new peers.

Joe has a 'stiff upper lip' approach to change. He doesn't allow himself to feel any trepidation but just gets on with it. He expects others to be vulnerable, and is accustomed to supporting his bosses rather than expecting support from them.

Bob doesn't feel his fear or scare either, but when he looks carefully at his reactions, he realises that his experience of endings is one of feeling almost unbearable grief and abandonment.

Jason was amazed and shocked to recognise how common it was for him to hurt himself at times of change. It tended to get him the attention and sympathy he craved.

NB: If you find doing these exercises distressing, stop and do some somatic resourcing (see Chapter 3). You might return to them with the support of a friend or counsellor.

WORKING WITH CLIENTS

We find the tasks of ending described by William Worden (2018) simple and yet powerful guidelines for attending to endings. We have adapted and elaborated them here, to suit the coaching context. At each task we suggest skills or interventions that the coach might find helpful.

The Tasks of Ending

1. Noticing That There is an Ending

This might seem like a very obvious task. It is easy to recognise an end if one has been made redundant or moved to a different company or lost a valued colleague. However, it is very common for an ending to go unrecognised in the context of an exciting new development in a person's career. Or if someone is in the thick of a challenging reorganisation or has taken on a new team member or secured a new much-desired promotion, the ending of the old might go unnoticed. It is surprising how important it is to recognise and name what is coming to an end. It is about appropriately honouring what has been before and making ready for the next. It is about living 'in the moment' (see Chapter 3). In terms of coaching, it is important that the coach refers to the ending long before it arrives. Unexpected endings are rarely useful. What is more, in a time-limited engagement, if the coach regularly mentions the up-coming ending – e.g., 'We are half way through our sessions,' or 'We have three more sessions,' or 'Next time will be our last session, so what still needs to be addressed?' – this can focus the client well and invite him to be more committed to what they might have perhaps avoided so far. Even in an ongoing coaching engagement, it is part of the work to notice and enquire into the client's patterns around ending and transitions, recognising if new skills or awareness might be usefully developed.

The Tasks of Ending

1. Recognise the existence of an ending or endings.
2. Recognise the significance of the ending and all its major and minor implications.
3. Stay with yourself, recognise how you feel and think about it.
4. Express it.
5. Plan for the future, including putting in place some of the important things identified in the second task – for example, where else to get the support you have experienced.
6. Mark the ending in some way.
7. Withdraw energy to reinvest in the future.

Figure 8.2 The Tasks of Ending (adapted from Worden, 2018)

2. Recognising the Significance of the Ending

As well as the obvious change, what other, perhaps minimised, losses or associations might be involved? For example, the new role in the organisation might come with a new office with a better view. But it may also mean saying goodbye to the secretary who has been so supportive, to the colleagues you had lunch with every day, to the journey to work because you are now located in head office in another part of the city, to the team drink on a Friday night, and so on.

In the example of John (above), it is easy to see that his new important role also involved loss of home and familiar surroundings – for him and also his Japanese wife. It meant a change in climate (the seasons can be very different in the UK and Japan), a change in colleagues, a change in living and working environment, a change in food and many other things. Also, at quite a deep level, it had a flavour of coming home – something he yearned for as a child and was tinged with not a little pain.

When the ending you are looking at is between the coach and the client, part of saying goodbye together will be to name the things that will be missing. Some of those might be desired – for example, the honouring of the completion of the contract and the achievement of the client's goals; the welcome loss of the traffic-laden car journey to the coaching venue, and so on. Some may need to be recognised and respected – for example, the loss of the supportive ear of someone who listens and does not judge; the loss of the two-hour period when the client could really slow down and take stock of where they are; the loss of the opportunity to think out loud and try on ideas without fear that people will immediately take their words and rush off to action them.

3. Recognising How You Feel about Ending and Finding a Way of Expressing It

Mostly, this is quite straight forward. Our clients can say how they feel about whatever goes with the transition. They can name it and say whether they are relieved or sad or indifferent or a bit of everything. But sometimes it is not so easy. If the coach senses that there is something getting in the way of the client's recognising and acknowledging, it can be useful to go through the core organisers, see what associations are being made and possibly find a way of finishing the 'unfinished business' from the past. Unfinished business is a term used especially by Gestaltists (Sills et al., 2012; Clarkson and Cavicchia 2013) who pay attention to the natural cycle of experience. This goes:

- the sensation and then recognition of a need stimulus or event;
- thinking and feeling about it, and mobilising energy;
- taking whole-hearted action and self-expression;
- completion and ultimate withdrawal of energy.

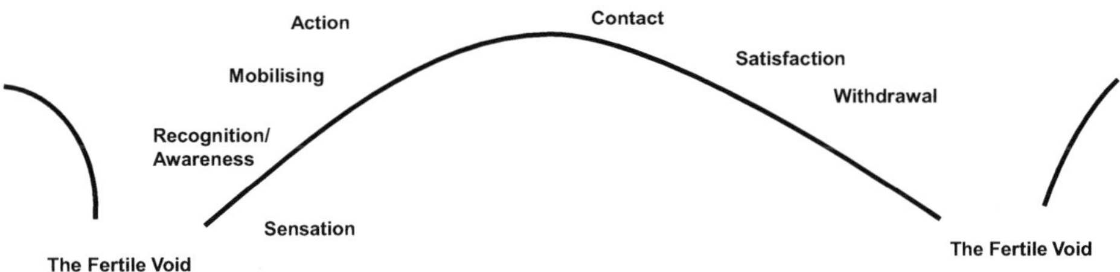

Figure 8.3 The Basic Cycle or Wave of Experience
Source: Adapted from Zinker (1977)

This is often expressed as a wave, to try to capture the natural flow of life (see Figure 8.3)

If the process gets interrupted at any stage – the feeling does not get expressed or the problem does not get resolved – it can lead to 'unfinished business'. The process of managing loss, endings and changes can frequently lead to unfinished business, as people minimise the importance of what they are going through. Equally, in childhood, parents can sometimes miss being attentive to their children's feelings about loss and change if they are very caught up in managing it themselves. In other words, challenging aspects of previous relationships, unacknowledged and unaddressed when they first occurred, can be carried into new relationships or situations whenever there is a transition, making it harder to form new and vibrant, up-to-date engagements. What is more, there is a risk of overly configuring the new relationship based on expectations from the past (see Chapter 5).

Example

As John shared his story, he recognised that much of the anxiety he felt about his competence in the new job was just a story to explain his feelings. There was an echo of the anxiety and loneliness he felt as a child. He had not been able to talk to anyone about his feelings and had bottled them up inside himself. The coach invited him to think about what 'young John' might have needed back then when he was nine years old. He said he would have wanted someone to put an arm round him and tell him, 'Don't worry, I will be here with you'.

The coach asked him:

C: Can you see that little boy in your mind's eye?
J: Yes – he's looking forlorn and little.
C: Will you close your eyes and imagine telling him that … what he needs to hear?
J: Closes eyes, pauses, then nods.
C: Did he hear you?
J: [Smiles] Yes, he did.
C: What's he doing now?

J: He is smiling. He looks relieved.
C: Just let him know that he can just sit with you. He doesn't have to do anything. You will manage the new job – it's not up to him.

John grins and nods with a dawning happiness.

4. Looking to the Future

Interestingly, it is a developmental achievement to be able to imagine what an unknown future may look like. A coach can help a client as far as possible to think about and plan for what the new situation will be like. This is easier in some cases where, for example, a client is making a shift to a new role within the present company or managing a number of relationships at different stages, as is often the case with work in matrix organisations. But if the change or ending is one where the future is not fully clear, which is often the case in twenty-first century organisational life, the model by Bridges and Bridges (2020) can be very supportive.

The Transition Model

William Bridges and his wife, Susan Bridges developed the Transition Model (see Figure 8.4) saying, 'Change is an event, but a transition is the *process* that you go through in response to the change'. The model has three stages: Endings, Neutral Zone and New Beginnings. They describe how the tasks outlined above are only the first stage of adjustment to change. Before the new chapter can begin, the person has to dwell in the 'neutral zone' for a while – especially if the new world is not clear. The coach can help the client plan for that, anticipate the disquiet of uncertainty and unfamiliarity that might arise, practice simply noticing and enquiring into their feelings, being willing to 'try on' new ideas or directions without rushing to choose one. This is also a time to take stock of what has been learned that can be carried forward into the new.

Another part of looking into the future and a task for the neutral zone – and beyond into new beginnings – is to think about where else the client might get some of what might be missing after the transition has happened, using the data from Task 2 above. For example, if what will be lost is a safe place to think aloud, where could the client establish that elsewhere? One client set up a small intimate peer group of other CEOs – colleagues and friends that they trusted. They would all meet every month or so for peer support and discussion. Another client decided to go for regular walks in the park where they could have the time and space to think that they had previously enjoyed on their train journeys to see their coach. The coach can help the client think about his needs – e.g., his bio-sociopsychological hungers as identified by Berne, 1964 – and how they can effectively be met in the client's new situation.

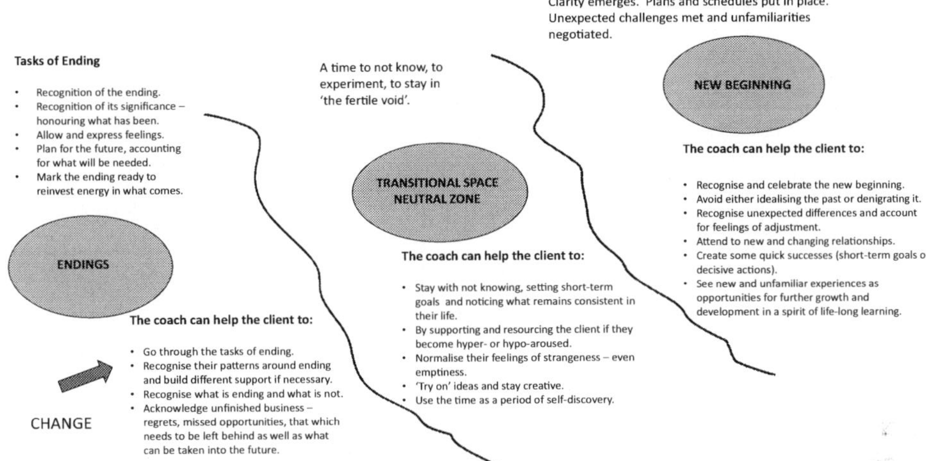

Figure 8.4 The Transition Model
Source: Adapted from Bridges (2020)

5. Letting Go of the Past, Ready to Reinvest Energy

The last of Worden's tasks is to be ready to step into the future whole-heartedly, without unfinished business. Once the 'right next step' is identified, we hope the client is ready to go into the New Beginning, knowing where to seek support and how to build the life they want.

CONCLUSION

We believe that paying careful attention to endings and transitions, honouring their significance and attending to our feelings about them, is a vital part of living healthily and fruitfully. We encourage coaches to think about, and work with, their own experiences and patterns around endings and changes in their lives, in order to be fully present to their clients and to help them, in their turn, make good endings and productive new beginnings. Each person's experience of the ending process – and indeed of any of the processes we discuss in this book – will be uniquely theirs. As Erv Polster said in the book of this title (1987), *Every Person's Life is Worth a Novel*, and the coach is in the privileged position of accompanying their client as they write it.

9

RELATIONSHIP AND RELATING AS A MORAL IMPERATIVE

HISTORY OF ETHICS IN COACHING

In Chapter 1, we described some ways in which the assumptions of individualism, positivism and modernism have shaped how organisations and their employees have been seen and thought about. Some of these assumptions have inevitably found their way into how coaching theory and practice have evolved. We compared scientific positivism and realism – with their assumption that there is an external reality that can be studied objectively – with more post-modern perspectives, such as social constructionism. Here, reality is seen as being constantly constructed and interpreted through multiple discourses and belief systems in ways that are not as neutral or objective as scientific positivism would suggest (Horkheimer, 1987; Gergen, 2009; Western, 2012). Throughout this book, we have explored how relational coaching embraces the fact of human subjectivity in both the coach and client, as well as in all those they interact with in their professional and personal lives.

Positivist assumptions about how the world is have given rise to a series of beliefs informing how questions of ethics have been traditionally approached in the helping professions. These have been summarised by Mattingly (2005) as:

1 It is possible to articulate universal, ethical principles or guidelines that are useful in every situation. Therefore, ethical rules are context free.
2 There is normally a 'right answer' in relation to whatever prevailing norms and principles are being used to guide ethical decision making.

3 There is an objective position from which to judge what one ought to do. The position is characterised by emotional detachment from the situation.
4 This objectively defined position, without any emotional involvement, enables the articulation of unambiguous, ethical guidelines.

These assumptions are also informed by individualism, the belief in individuals being isolated and self-serving, which calls for codes for guiding the activities and types of relationships of people who as Hinman (2008, cited in Carrol and Shaw, 2013) 'neither know or care about one another' (p. 269). Carrol and Shaw (2013) describe how in the individualist tradition of moral philosophy the concept of relationship is only considered through the lens of social contract theory. This theory proposes that human beings are independent agents, driven by self-interest, who choose to subject themselves to rules that ensure that all derive some benefits.

Hinman (2008) goes on to describe how the traditions of moral philosophy, which inform many principles and codes of ethics, have not considered relationships, relational contexts, or valued subjectivity. Instead, they have tended to emphasise reason and denied any personal connection to the questions of ethics. Feminist philosophers, particularly Carol Gilligan (1982), have argued powerfully that the perspective of social contract theory, with its view of individuals as stripped of emotion and wedded to logic and reason, dismisses those qualities that constitute our very humanity (Carrol and Shaw, 2013). This is further supported by perspectives from evolutionary psychology and neuroscience that demonstrate the critical role of emotions in shaping how we think and the behaviours our thoughts give rise to (Damasio, 2010).

A RELATIONAL ORIENTATION

A relational orientation to coaching emphasises the fundamental and inevitable interconnectedness of human beings and therefore highlights the importance of how people take into account the influences and requirements of relational responsibility, fairness, justice and connectedness (Gilligan, 1982). It raises questions such as how do we balance what we owe ourselves with what we owe others. Carrol and Shaw (2013) stress that without this relational orientation and attention to relational factors 'many important elements are lost, decision making may be flawed or inadequate, and implementation of good decisions may flounder' (p. 104).

They argue that for too long codes and frameworks (informed by the assumptions set out above) have been used as the only criteria for determining competency in ethical decision making. These documents, as argued by Pope and

Vasquez (2007, cited in Carrol and Shaw, 2013), cannot be a substitute for active, engaged, deliberate and creative approaches to fulfilling ethical responsibility. Rules can offer a degree of guidance but are insufficient in dealing with the complexities of everyday life and the VUCA (volatile, uncertain, complex and ambiguous) world:

> there will always be too many exceptions to the rules in the shape of particular circumstances and complicating details. Therefore, there is a need for concepts and navigational tools that will assist organizational members in unique situations, which can be understood in different ways and often involve many conflicting considerations.
>
> (Haslebo and Haslebo, 2012, p. 28)

Once we take seriously the vital role of context in shaping and influencing human emotions, thinking and behaviour, we discover that what might be considered unethical in one context could be justifiable in another. The ethical maturity needed in today's complex environments, involves individuals (including coaches and clients and their institutions) seeing themselves as participating in co-creating narratives, realities and behaviours, rather than relying on prior certainties and assumptions.

This does not, however, imply moral relativism where any action can be justified. There are still important principles required to guide ethical decision making in complex contexts.

FROM ETHICAL COMPETENCE TO ETHICAL MATURITY

Transformational learning and adult vertical development (Kegan, 1994; Laloux, 2014) demonstrate that, as adults mature and expand their meaning-making perspectives, overreliance on rigid rules gives way to being guided more by principles. They can embrace a perception of reality that is more complex, where answers to difficult problems and ethical dilemmas need to be discovered on a case-by-case, situation-by-situation basis. This takes relational coaches beyond the territory of ethical pseudo-competence into the territory of ethical maturity involving:

> the reflective, rational, emotional and intuitive capacity to decide actions are right and wrong, or good and better; the resilience and courage to implement those decisions; the willingness to be accountable for ethical

> decisions made (publicly or privately); and the ability to learn from and live with the experience.
>
> (Carrol and Shaw, 2013, p. 3)

Writing from within the social-constructionist paradigm, Haslebo and Haslebo (2012) consider a relational approach to ethics as involving abandoning universal definitions of 'true and false', 'good and bad', 'right and wrong', and orienting more to exploring and studying consciously how individuals co-construct meaning, co-ordinating their actions and patterns of relating. They identify what they see as five core concepts that can be used to shed light on these processes. Each has ethical implications for practice.

1. Context

This is concerned with how in societies and organisations meaning is co-created in unpredictable ways that can never fully be understood by any one individual given the multiple variables and perspectives at play. If we let this principle inform our thinking, this gives rise to a 'moral obligation' (Haslebo and Haslebo, 2012, p. 34), which Haslebo and Haslebo see as a social responsibility based on embracing the idea that as humans we are not simply *subjected to* events but also *participate in* creating these events.

We are co-responsible for creating situations in which all involved can contribute constructively. This has implications for the responsibility coaches and clients have for co-creating the work and outcomes, as well as exploring the role each plays in shaping the organisations and societies in which the coaching is taking place. It is for this reason that in our teaching we often ask coaches to think about the ethical principles underpinning their practice and the types of contexts and organisations they may find problematic (see Level 1 of the Levels of Contract in Chapter 2).

2. Relationship

Drawing on the work of linguistic philosopher John Austin (1962) who demonstrates the relationship building power of language, as well as the work of narrative-based anthropological research which shows how words take their meaning from their cultural context, Haslebo and Haslebo (2012) identify a particular moral compass point which they call 'the obligation to engage in dialogue' (p. 35). For coaches, this implies the need to be alert to the ways in which meaning is being made in the coaching relationship and context, and to be willing to explore and question where necessary the efficacy and impacts of these processes.

3. Discourse

This relates to how discourses – the ways in which meaning is made, shaped by culture and history – inform the narratives that operate in organisations and societies. These narratives define and support particular positions and possibilities while limiting others. They determine the roles that individuals are expected to take up, such as leader and follower, manager and employee, in-crowd and out-crowd, heroes, villains and victims, and so forth.

These narratives become like scripts in a play, with set characters and specific scenes, which tightly bind the field of possibility and do not facilitate the creation of new ways of thinking about, and responding to, today's complex challenges (for more on 'script', see Chapter 5). The moral and ethical responsibility here is for the coach and client to pay close attention to how these discourses shape the positions that individuals place themselves in (including coach, client and other individuals in their relevant context). It calls for coach and client to assume shared responsibility for ensuring positioning that can contribute to respectful relationships, individual and organisational creativity and flourishing. As a result of this particular moral imperative, coaches may choose to question the dominant discourses in a client's organisation. These discourses may be limiting an individual and/or the organisation from developing new forms of thinking, relating and acting that might be required to respond effectively to the challenges and complexity of the VUCA world, and social and environmental responsibility.

4. Value

Drawing on the work of Dewey (1916) and philosopher Axel Honneth (1995), Haslebo and Haslebo highlight the importance of recognition for human beings in order to feel of worth and value. This gives rise to the moral obligation which they call 'inquiry of value to the work community' (2012, p. 224). It involves holding in mind the question of how one's own and others' positions and actions can be of value to the whole work community, wider society and planetary ecosystem. For coaches, this raises questions about the position they take in relation to the impact their work and the organisations they work in might be having on societies and the planet, the type of work contexts they choose to engage in, and in service of what they choose to engage. It is important that coaches monitor their feelings and choices in relation to the work they undertake and the industries and sectors they work in. Any internal conflicts and ambivalence they might feel are likely to find their way into the dynamics of the coaching relationship and affect the work and its outcomes.

5. Power

Different individuals in societies and organisations do not have the same opportunities for having their voices heard and contributing to contexts that are creative and constructive. This introduces the moral obligation of helping to create possibilities where leaders and followers, those above in the hierarchy and those below, might come together in mutually respectful relationships, assuming shared responsibility for the cultures, behaviours and strategies they create. This points to a need for coaches to be willing to explore questions of power with their clients, how they are both enabled and constrained by it, and also find strategies for unlocking, where possible, the collective intelligence of everyone in an organisation.

This is a characteristic feature of post conventional organisations (Laloux, 2014) that recognise that the capacity to lead and follow, depending on individual talent and experience, is not solely related to an individual's position in an organisational hierarchy. This is important for innovation, and generating creativity and flexibility for responding to problems that cannot be resolved by relying on conventional paradigms and historical assumptions about roles.

Relational Concepts, Moral Obligations and Implications for Practice

1. Context

As humans, we have social responsibility because we are not simply subjected to events but also participate in creating these events.

The coach will:

- Be concerned with the ways in which the coaching – its goals and focus – contribute to creating conditions in which the client, those they interact with and the organisations they participate in, can make constructive contributions in their immediate and wider contexts.
- Offer perspectives on possible implications of the coaching and invite the client to consider their intentions and impact beyond their immediate individual goals and objectives.

2. Relationship

We have an obligation to engage in dialogue because language takes its meaning from its particular content and moment in time.

The coach will:

- Pay attention to the language they, their clients and others in their context use and the meanings that language carries in these contexts.
- Actively invite clients to reframe existing language and meanings where this might be necessary to expand perspective.
- Be alert to and name language and attitudes that reinforce individualist assumptions and beliefs that result in treating others as objects to be manipulated rather than subjects.
- Make use of their differences and subjective uniqueness to introduce differences of perspective without attachment to being right or trying to convince the client. This way both coach and client engage in a democratic process where both stand to change perspective if they so wish.

3. Discourse

As the way in which meaning is made is shaped by culture and history, we have a moral obligation to examine the ensuing narratives that operate in organisations, communities and societies.

The coach will:

- Consider with the client ways in which culture, history and context shape the assumptions and meanings people hold about 'how things are done around here' and 'how I need to be to be part of this system'.
- Surface and reflect on assumptions and consider ways in which they might support or restrict respectful relationships, individual and organisational creativity and flourishing.
- Explore with the client the ways these narratives and untested assumptions shape their feelings, emotional range, thoughts and actions. Invite experiment (see Chapter 7) with new ways of thinking and acting when existing patterns are considered to be limiting in some way.

4. Value

We have a moral obligation to consider how coaching can be affirming of individual clients, and how its impacts can be of value to the wider system and society.

The coach will:

- Respect, affirm and appreciate the intrinsic worth of the client as a fellow human being.
- Explore with the client how their feelings, thoughts and actions might be of value in their local context, as well as influence further afield.

- Respectfully draw attention to feelings, thoughts and actions (or inactions) that might cause harm to individuals and groups.

5. Power

We have a moral obligation of helping to create opportunities for the powerful and less powerful to come together in mutually respectful relationships, assuming shared responsibility for the cultures, behaviours and strategies they create.

The coach will:

- Explore with clients their experience of power in themselves and others in their context.
- Explore ways in which the positions they and others take in relation to power – formally and informally – both enable and constrain them and others.
- Explore common constructions of power such as hierarchy and the patterns of feeling, thinking, relating and acting these give rise to.
- Experiment with shifts in feeling, thinking and acting in order to reduce any negative implications of the way power operates for themselves and their clients.

The perspectives we have been setting out in this book point to a world that is far more complex than traditional assumptions about organisations and ethics might suggest. They call for an approach to ethics that moves away from universal principles and guidelines to what Mattingly (2005) terms a 'narrative ethics', whose main objective is to discover what constitutes the 'good' in each unique and specific situation. From a social constructionist perspective, this requires us to explore what stories individuals (including the coach) see themselves as being part of, the network of relationships they consider themselves to be situated within (as in Western's (2013) network discourse), and what future they are trying to build.

One of the areas in which ethical questions arise is in the context of the coach and client's relationship to one another and the context in which they are working. As relational coaching embraces the inevitable subjectivity of all parties involved in the coaching engagement – including the sponsor, coach, client and wider system in which the coaching is taking place – individuals are often involved in a process of negotiating and meaning-making in relation to differences and similarities in feeling, thinking and behaviour. A fundamental dilemma for each of us is, on one hand, the need for security and belonging in predictability – *common* languages, assumptions and meanings – and, on the other, the need to have our *individual experiential uniqueness* acknowledged and allowed expression.

As Keith Tudor (2025) says:

> the experience and task of the individual human being may be summarised as negotiating a need to be separate or different, and to connect and belong, in the face of difference, diversity, and adversity. In this sense, difference and diversity are not problems but existential realities and necessary opportunities. It's the problem we make of difference that's often the problem.

From the perspective of individual and organisational learning and change, exploring different subjectivities and constructions relative to dominant and enduring patterns of meaning and behaviour is key to transformation and innovation – yet it can be difficult to do.

Individuals in any social system or context are faced with a series of personal tensions. On one hand, how much to join with the prevailing ideology, culture and norms of the context, thereby experiencing being part of something, being heard and included, while simultaneously compromising their sense of autonomy and individuality. On the other, how much to question or stand separate and apart, thereby asserting their difference and potentially compromising their sense of being part of something (and risking ejection if this difference is too marked).

Gestalt (Wheeler, 2000; Clarkson and Cavicchia, 2013; Joyce and Sills, 2018) offers a very useful way of thinking about how individuals relate to one another and the environment. It works on a continuum from *confluence* (where an individual and the environment are almost identical as in the case of individuals who go along with whatever another person thinks and says, or swallow whole and without question an organisation's norms, culture and ways of working) to *isolation* (where an individual sees and experiences themselves as completely separate and different from others and the organisation). Coaches will also position themselves in or out of awareness somewhere on this continuum with different clients and contexts. This gives rise to a number of possible relational patterns. Cavicchia and Gilbert (2018) have taken this continuum of isolation and confluence, and applied it to coaching and organisational life.

- Coach and/or client are oriented towards merger.
- Can reflect early *anxious/preoccupied* attachment style.
- Unexamined and often unconscious introjection of organisational requirements and expectations.
- Environment dominates with no room for different individual perspectives - no 'mind of one's own'.
- Group think and compliance.
- Client and/or coach does and thinks what is required by environment – 'drinking the Kool Aid'.
- Ego ideal and organisational ideal are one and the same.
- Organisation's needs and expectations are privileged by coach and coachee in the contracting.

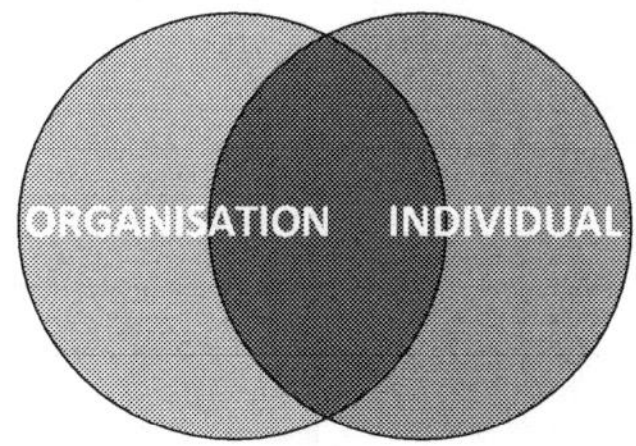

Figure 9.1 Implications of a Relational Stance of Confluence

- Client and/or coach are orientated towards separateness from the organisation, isolation.
- Can reflect early *avoidant* attachment patterns.
- Identity defined in contrasting me–not me.
- Individual without environment – isolated mind, closed system.
- Individualistic and possibly self-serving.
- Client may struggle to make necessary and reasonable compromises in order to be part of, and get along with others in, the system.
- Coach likely to focus on coachee and be less oriented towards the organisation's context, requirements and position in the multipointed contract.

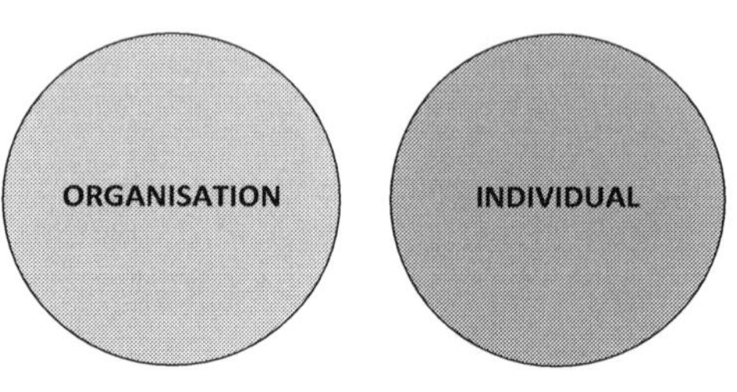

Figure 9.2 Implications of a Relational Stance of Isolation

- Coach and/or coachee simultaneously aware of their individual boundaries and preferences and the organisation's dynamics and requirements.
- Associated with secure attachment style.
- Conscious reflection and negotiation at the boundary between individual and organisation.
- Choiceful and aware compromising.
- Choiceful and aware challenge and push back from individual when 'required' compromises lead to a threat to individual integrity.
- Collaboration.
- 'Selfing' – individual and organisation reciprocally shape one another.
- Innovation, evolution, adaptation.

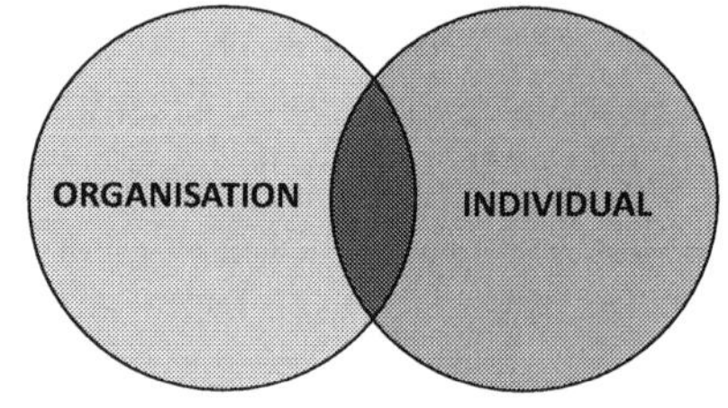

Figure 9.3 Implications of a Relational Stance of Contact

Contact in Gestalt is where an individual does not meet the environment from either extreme pole of confluence or isolation, but rather can hold the tension between these polarities and experience simultaneously their degree of sameness with the other person or the environment and culture of the organisation, as well as their degrees of difference. This allows an individual to both experience degrees of connection and feeling part of something, along with degrees of uniqueness and difference. It supports the paradoxical needs we all have to belong and have our uniqueness valued. It is the position of contact that best supports coaches and their clients to explore similarities and differences between them and the organisational context. It enables them to think together about any ethical issues that may arise and how the coach and client may need at times to lean into confluence or assert difference where they may feel compromised in some way. In fact, contact offers a model of relating likely to support a more democratic process in individuals and their systems which can include plurality in the form of different subjectivities and perspectives and protect the space for exploration, mutual interest and discovery.

One of the key areas for exploration and collaborative enquiry in a relational orientation to coaching is what happens for individuals in their context.

Exercise 9.1

On Your Own

Surfacing Relational Ethical Forces

The following questions are useful for helping coaches and their clients explore the ethical tensions that come into focus in a relational orientation. This is not an exhaustive list and the questions do not have 'once and for all' answers, rather they are designed to support ongoing enquiry into the ethical underpinnings of any coaching engagement. It is also important to remember that the coach and client may differ in their responses to these questions.

Relationship to the Organisation

Notice how you respond to the following questions. It may well be that your response leads to more questions rather than answers and in some ways this is inevitable, even desirable, as mature, relational ethical practice needs to be an ongoing enquiry into ourselves, our clients and the wider networks we inhabit. Our actions cannot but have consequences, whether we are aware of them or not.

- How do the context, culture and established ways of working in the organisation inform you and your client's sense of self, feelings, thinking and behaviour?
- What do you feel and think about the implications of this?
- At any time, to what extent do you and/or your client find yourselves aligning with or standing separate from an organisation's norms, culture, purpose and ways of working?
- How do you experience the requirements of role and situation?
- How do you and your different clients manage the boundary between your sense of personal self and role identity?
- How does this then give rise to the particular ways in which you and your client feel, think and act in response?
- To what extent does this way of being support health and growth while balancing individual needs and organisation requirements?
- What compromises are you and your different clients willing, in different contexts, to make consciously in order to go on being part of an organisation?
- What requirements of context, choices, expectations and behaviour make functional compromising impossible because they result in you or your client(s) feeling compromised in your ethical and moral integrity?
- What do you and your client(s) do when this happens?

We are finding that increasingly clients bring to coaching questions and dilemmas associated with these processes. Once you have explored these questions so that you understand their significance 'from the inside out' you might find them useful for enquiring with your client about their stance.

In this chapter we have explored the complexities and subtle challenges of a relational approach to ethics, both as an individual and in an organisational context. We discussed how a relational approach moves away from the idea that there is one constant truth or 'right' way and towards the notion that context changes everything – context in terms of times, place, space and cultural norms. We offer a model, based on Gestalt theory to elaborate the multilayered nature of beliefs and attitudes.

It may seem strange to be discussing ethics in the very last chapter of the book when it is evident that an ethical stance is key to safe and effective coaching from the first moment of meeting. We hope that the reader will have sensed that ethics are the framework and guide to all coaching skills. We decided to leave an in-depth exploration to the end of the book for two reasons. The first is so that we can refer meaningfully to the content of the foregoing chapters in order to link what we are saying to practice. The second is that we see ethical thinking and being as a major part of what the world needs from us in the troubled times of the twenty-first century.

CONCLUDING THOUGHTS: 'THE RAFT OF THE MEDUSA'

It is a wonderful feature of the dialogic, collaborative enquiry process at the heart of relational coaching that new insights, thoughts and images 'appear' unbidden as a result of the coach and client becoming interested in one another. Working together on this book, towards the end of the writing process, one of us suddenly, and quite unexpectedly, remembered a painting by the artist Théodore Géricault (1791–1824) that they had seen in the Louvre many years ago, called 'Le Radeau de la Méduse' ('The Raft of the Medusa'). It portrays a group of individuals clinging desperately to a makeshift raft following the wreck of a French naval frigate, the *Méduse* (https://collections.louvre.fr/en/ark:/53355/cl010059199).

As we pondered why, at this stage in writing a book on relational coaching skills, this arresting image should show up, we found ourselves thinking together about the desperate and troubling times in which we are currently living. At the time of writing, there are several major wars raging in the world; the United Kingdom continues to make sense of the implications of Brexit and severing relationships with mainland Europe; an attempt is being made to pass legislation in the UK to deport to Rwanda refugees literally arriving on rafts across the Channel; we are experiencing great geopolitical instability and existential threats, not only from the possibility of escalating international hostilities, but also the climate emergency, the evidence for which increases daily.

Cavicchia and Gilbert (2018) describe how we are also experiencing 'seismic shifts' (p. 3) in belief systems such as the social construction of ethnicity, power, sex, organisational theory and capitalism. Increasingly, the shadows of market forces are being aired on an unprecedented scale in the global arena, such as how the greatest wealth is held by a tiny fraction of the world's population. They go on to demonstrate connections between these realities and the individualistic and modernist ideologies that have governed patterns of human behaviour for centuries. To varying degrees, these ideologies have privileged seeing human beings as isolated individuals needing to extract resources and compete in order to survive.

This individual, self-oriented and self-serving bias is also a feature of the psychological process known as narcissism. Here, in order to defend against shame-inducing feelings of emptiness and vulnerability (Cavicchia, 2012), individuals construct and cling to grandiose self-images and identities based on power, superiority, status, attractiveness, success, etc. much like the survivors of the *Méduse* to their raft. These egoic identities need constant shoring up through the acquisition of symbols of status and the manipulation and exploitation of others who, instead of being related to as subjects, with minds, needs, vulnerabilities and desires of their own, are related to as objects to be used. On reading more about the wreck of the *Méduse*, we discovered that the survivors resorted to cannibalism, devouring one another in an attempt to survive.

Against this backdrop of instability, anxiety and vulnerability, it seems to us that the case for a relational orientation to living, being, organising and coaching is stronger than ever. As Cavicchia and Gilbert (2018) point out, the bias of individualism leads people to manage their anxieties by rigidifying their existing beliefs, retreating into 'individual isolation, or tightly policed homogenised groups, where membership is predicated on unquestioning compliance with groupthink, community and organisational norms' (p. 4). This takes us dangerously in the direction of fascism and totalitarianism, amplifying competition for ever dwindling resources and cannibalising our fragile ecosystem upon which our survival truly depends. All too slowly are societies and organisations starting to recognise some of the impact that white supremacy has had – and continues to have – on the global south.

On a more hopeful note, uncertainty, instability and disorientation provide opportunities to question and free ourselves from the constraining elements of past constructs that are revealing themselves to be, at best, unreliable in conferring order and stability, and at worst, overly limiting and even harmful. The outcome research we have referenced amply demonstrates the fundamental interconnectedness of humanity and the potential of working together in relationship to learn, expand perspective and human potential. As a relational and social species, we *do* have the potential to come together, listen, empathise, make meaning and strategise for collective survival and well-being. In this book we have set out some guidance for how we might approach this daunting yet vital necessity.

REFERENCES

Ainsworth, M. D. and Bell, S. M. (1970). Attachment, exploration, and separation: Illustrated by the behavior of one-year-olds in a strange situation. *Child Development*, 41 (1): 49–67.

Ainsworth, M.D.S., Blehar, M.C., Waters, E. and Wall, S. (1978) *Patterns of Attachments: A Psychological Study of the Strange Situation.* Hillsdale, NJ: Lawrence Erlbaum Associates.

Allen, J.R. (2000) 'Biology and transactional analysis II: a status report on neurodevelopment', *Transactional Analysis Journal*, 30 (4): 260–9.

Aron, L. (1991) 'The patient's experience of the analyst's subjectivity', *Psychoanalytic Dialogues*, 1 (1).

Asay, T.P. and Lambert, M.J. (1999) 'The empirical case for the common factors in therapy: quantitative findings'. In M.A. Hubble, B.L. Duncan and S.D. Miller (eds), *The Heart and Soul of Change: What Works in Therapy.* Washington, DC: APA Press, pp. 33–56.

Austin, J.L. (1962) *How to do Things with Words.* New York: Oxford University Press.

Bachkirova, T. (2016) 'The self of the coach: conceptualization, issues and opportunities for practitoner development', *Consulting Psychology Journal: Practice and Research*, 68 (2).

Balick, A. (2014) *The Psychodynamics of Social Networking: Connected up Instaneous Culture and the Self.* London: Routledge.

Baptiste-Grant, J., Sills, C. and Bell, J. (2024 in progress) *Authenticity, Courage and Race in Coaching.*

Beisser, A.R. (1970) 'The paradoxical theory of change'. In J. Fagan and I. Shepherd (eds), *Gestalt Therapy Now.* Palo Alto, CA: Science and Behaviour, pp. 77–80.

Berne, E. (1961) *Transactional Analysis in Psychotherapy.* New York: Grove Press.

Berne, E. (1964/2010) *Games People Play.* New York: Grove Press/London: Penguin.

Berne, E. (1966) *Principles of Group Treatment.* New York: Oxford University Press.

Berne, E. (1972/1974) *What Do You Say after You Say Hello?: The Psychology of Human Destiny.* New York: Grove Press.

Bordin, E.S. (1979) 'The generalizability of the psychoanalytic concept of the working alliance', *Psychotherapy: Theory, Research and Practice*, 16 (3): 252–60.

Bordin, E.S. (1994) 'Theory and research on the therapeutic working alliance'. In O. Horvath and J. Greenberg (eds), *The Working Alliance: Theory Research and Practice* New York: Wiley, pp. 13–37.

Boston Change Process Study Group (2007) 'The Something More Than Interpretation Revisited: Sloppiness and Co-Creativity in the Psychoanalytic Encounter', *Int. Journal of Psychoanalysis* 88: 1–16.

Boston Change Process Study Group (2010) *Change in Psychotherapy: A Unifying Paradigm*. New York: Norton.

Bowlby, J. (1969) *Attachment and Loss, Vol. 1: Attachment*. London: Hogarth Press and the Institute of Psychoanalysis.

Bowlby, J. (1973) *Attachment and Loss, Vol. 2: Separation – Anxiety and Anger*. London: Hogarth Press and the Institute of Psychoanalysis.

Bridges, W. with Bridges, S. (2020) *Transitions* (40th anniversary edition). Da Capo Lifelong Books.

Buber, M. (1965) *Between Man and Man*. New York: Macmillan.

Burr, V. (2003) *Social Constructionism*. London: Routledge.

Carrol, M. and Shaw, E. (2013) *Ethical Maturity in the Helping Professions: Making Difficult Life and Work Decisions*. Philadelphia, PA: Jessica Kingsley Publishers.

Cavanagh, M. (2006) 'Coaching from a systemic perspective: a complex adaptive conversation'. In D.R. Stober and A.M. Grant (eds), *Evidence Based Coaching Handbook*. Wiley.

Cavanagh, M. (2013) 'The coaching engagement in the twenty-first century: new paradigms for complex times'. In S. David, D. Clutterbuck and D. Megginson (eds), *Beyond Goals: Effective Strategies for Coaching and Mentoring*. Aldershot: Gower.

Cavicchia, S. (2012) 'Shame in the coaching relationship'. In E. De Haan and C. Sills (eds), *Coaching Relationships: The Relational Coaching Fieldbook*. London: Libri.

Cavicchia, S. and Gilbert, M. (2018) *The Theory and Practice of Relational Coaching: Complexity, Paradox and Integration*. London: Routledge.

Chidiac, M.-A. and Denham-Vaughan, S. (2007) 'The process of presence: energetic availability and fluid responsiveness', *British Gestalt Journal*, 16 (1): 9–19.

Choy, A. (1990) 'The winner's triangle', *Transactional Analysis Journal*, 20 (1): 40–6.

Clarkson, P. (1995) *The Therapeutic Relationship*. 2nd edition. London: Whurr Publishers.

Clarkson, P. and Cavicchia, S. (2013) *Gestalt Counselling in Action*. London: Sage.

Clemmens, M. (2011) 'The interactive field: Gestalt therapy as an embodied relational dialogue'. In T. Bar-Yoseph (ed.), *Gestalt Therapy: Advances in Theory and Practice*. London: Routledge.

Clemmens, M. and Bursztyn, A. (2003) 'Culture and body', *British Gestalt Journal*, 12 (1): 15–21.

Cook-Greuter, S. (2004) 'Making the case for developmental perspective', *Industrial and Commercial Training*, 36: 275–81.

Cozolino, Louis J. (2016) *Why Therapy Works: using our minds to change our brains*. New York: W.W. Norton & Company.

Critchley, B. (2021) *Letters to a Leader: Twelve Lessons in Being a Leader*. Oxford: Libri Publishing.

Damasio, A. (2010) *Self Comes to Mind: Constructing the Social Brain*. New York: Random House.

Day, A. (2019) *Disruption, Change and Transformation in Organisations: A Human Relations Perspective*. London: Routledge.

De Haan, E. (2021) *What Works in Executive Coaching: Understanding Outcomes through Quantitative Research and Practice-based Evidence*. London/New York: Routledge.

De Haan, E. and C. Sills (eds) (2012) *Coaching Relationships: The Relational Coaching Fieldbook*. London: Libri.

De Haan, E., Grant, A. Burger, Y. and Eriksson, P-O. (2016) 'A large scale study of executive and workplace coaching: the relative contributions of relationship, personality match, and self-efficacy', *Consulting Psychology Journal: Practice and Research*. American Psychological Association, 68 (3): 189–207.

Denham, J. (2006) 'The presence of the trainer', *British Gestalt Journal*, 15 (1): 16–22.

Denham-Vaughan, S. (2005) 'Will and grace', *British Gestalt Journal*, 14 (1): 5–14.

Dewey, J. (1916) *Democracy and Education*. New York: The Free Press.

Duncan, B.L. (2014) *On Becoming a Better Therapist: Evidence Based Practice One Client at a Time*. Washington: APA.

Dusay, J. (1966) 'Response to games in therapy', *Transactional Analysis Bulletin*, 5 (18): 136–7.

Eisenstein, C. (2011) *Sacred Economics: Money, Gift and Society in the Age of Transition*. Evolver Editions.

Eisenstein, C. (2013) *The More Beautiful World Our Hearts Know is Possible*. Berkeley, CA: North Atlantic Books.

English, F. (1975) 'The three-cornered contract', *Transactional Analysis Bulletin*, 5 (4): 383–4. doi:10.1177/036215377500500413

Flückiger, C., DelRe, A.C., Wampold, B.E. and Horvath, A.O. (2017) 'Alliance meta-analysis 2017: symptom specificity & alliance outcome correlation'. Paper presented at the Society for Psychotherapy Research, Toronto.

Fogel, A. (2009) *Body Sense: The Science and Practice of Embodied Self Awareness*. New York: W.W. Norton.

Foucault, M. (1983) 'Discourse and truth: the problematization of parrhesia' (six lectures). The University of California at Berkeley.

Freud, S. (1950/1914) *Erinnern, Wiederholen und Durcharbeiten* ('Remembering, repeating and working-through'), Vol. 12 of Standard Edition.

Friston, K. (2010). 'The free-energy principle: a unified brain theory?'. *Nature Reviews Neuroscience*. 11 (2): 127–138. doi:10.1038/nrn2787. PMID 20068583. S2CID 5053247 (accessed 9 July 2023).

Gendlin, E. (1997) *Experiencing and the Creation of Meaning: A Philosophical and Psychological Approach to the Subjective*. Northwestern University Press (first published 1962, The Free Press of Glencoe).

Gergen, K.J. (1985) 'The social constructionist movement in modern psychology', *American Psychologist*, 40: 266–75.

Gergen, K.J. (2009) *Relational Being*. Oxford: Oxford University Press.

Gilbert, M. and Orlans, V. (2010) *Integrative Psychotherapy: 100 Key Points*. London: Routledge.

Gilchrist, I. (2010) *The Master and his Emissary*. Newhaven, CT: Yale University Press.

Gilligan, C. (1982) *In a Different Voice: Psychological Theory and Women's Development*. Cambridge, MA: Harvard University Press.

Hanson, R. (2011) 'How to take in the good'. Greater Good Science Center. Available at: https://greatergood.berkeley.edu/video/item/how_to_take_in_the_good (accessed 27 August 2024).

Hargaden, H. and Sills, C. (2002) *Transactional Analysis: A Relational Perspective.* London: Routledge.

Hart, A. (2018) 'Can we bear to turn our psychotherapeutic attention toward those who are other?' Keynote speech at the annual conference of the International Association of Relational Transactional Analysis.

Hart, A. (2018/2020) 'The case for radical openness: mind of state'. Available at: https://mindofstate.com/the-case-for-radical-openness/ (accessed 26 August 2024).

Haslebo, G. and Haslebo, M.L. (2012) *Practicing Relational Ethics in Organizations.* Chagrin Falls, OH: Taos Institute Publications.

Heron, J., & Reason, P. (1997). *A Participatory Inquiry Paradigm. Qualitative Inquiry,* 3(3), 274–294. https://doi.org/10.1177/107780049700300302

Heron, J. (2001) *Helping the Client.* London: Sage.

Hill, R. (2024, in press) *Telling the Truth: The Therapist's Dilemma.* London: Karnac.

Hinman, L.M. (2008) *Ethics: A Pluralistic Approach to Moral Theory* (4th edn). Boston, MA: Thomson Wadsworth.

Hirshhorn, L. (1998) *Reworking Authority: Leading and Following in the Post-Modern Organization.* Cambridge, MA: The MIT Press.

Hirschhorn, L. and Barnett, C. (eds) (1993) *The Psychodynamics of Organizations.* Philadelphia, PA: Temple University Press.

Honneth, A. (1995) *The Struggle for Recognition: The Moral Grammar of Social Conflicts.* Cambridge, MA: The MIT Press.

Horkheimer, E. (1987) *The Eclipse of Reason.* Boston, MA: Beacon Press.

Horvath, A.O. (2018) 'Research on the alliance: knowledge in search of a theory', *Psychotherapy Research*, 28 (4): 499–516. doi:10.1080/10503307.2017.1373204

Horvath, A.O. and Symonds, B.D. (1991) 'Relation between working alliance and outcome in psychotherapy: a meta-analysis', *Journal of Counseling Psychology*, 38: 139–49.

Horvath, A.O. and Greenberg, L.S. (eds) (1994) *The Working Alliance: Theory Research and Practice.* New York: Wiley, pp. 13–37.

Jacobs, L. (2017) 'Hopes, fears and enduring relational themes', *British Gestalt Journal*, 25 (1): 6–16.

Joyce, P. and Sills, C. (2018) *Skills in Gestalt Counselling and Psychotherapy* (4th edn). London: Sage.

Joyce, P. and Sills, C. (2023) 'Domains of Self Disclosure', *Model developed for Gestalt Psychotherapy Training Programme.*

Kahler, T. (1975) 'Drivers: the key to the process of scripts', *Transactional Analysis Journal*, 5 (3): 280–4.

Kahler, T. and Capers, H. (1974) 'The miniscript', *Trans-actionalAnalysis Journal*, 4 (1): 26–42.

Kant, I. (1965) *Critique of Pure Reason* (translated by N.K. Smith from original published 1781). New York: St Martin's Press.

Karpman, S. (1968) 'Fairy tales and script drama analysis', *Transactional Analysis Bulletin*, 7 (26): 39–43.

Kegan, R. (1994) *In Over Our Heads: The Mental Demands of Modern Life*. Cambridge, MA: Harvard University Press.

Kline, N. (2002) *Time to Think: Listening to Ignite the Human Mind*. London: Cassell.

Laloux, F. (2014) *Reinventing Organizations: A Guide to Organizations Inspired by the Next Stage of Human Consciousness*. Nelson Parker.

Lapworth, P. and Sills, C. (2011) *Integration in Counselling and Psychotherapy*. London: Sage.

Leary-Joyce, J. (2014) *The Fertile Void: Gestalt Coaching at Work*. AOEC Press.

Levinas, E. (1989) (ed. S. Hand) *The Levinas Reader*. Oxford: Blackwell.

Lévi-Strauss, C. (1968) *The Savage Mind (La Pensée Sauvage)*. Chicago: Chicago University Press.

Lewin, R. and Regine, B. (2001) *Weaving Complexity and Business: Engaging the Soul at Work*. New York: Texere.

Little, R. (2006) 'Ego state relational units and resistence to change', *Transactional Analysis Journal*, 36: 7–19.

Luborsky, L., Singer, B. and Luborsky, L. (1975) 'Comparative studies of psychotherapies', *Archives of General Psychiatry*, 32: 995–1008.

Main, M. (1995) 'Recent studies in attachment: overview, with selected implications for clinical work'. In S. Goldberg, R. Muir and J. Kerr (eds), *Attachment Theory: Social, Developmental, and Clinical Perspectives*. Hillsdale, NJ: Analytic Press, pp. 407–74.

Main, M., Kaplan, N. and Cassidy, J. (1965) 'Security in Infancy, Childhood, and Adulthood: A Move to the Level of Representation'. *Growing Points of Attachment Theory and Research*, 50 1(2): 66–104.

Martin, D.J., Garske, J.P. and Davis, M.K. (2000) 'Relation of the therapeutic alliance with outcome and other variables: a meta-analytic review', *Journal of Consulting and Clinical Psychology*, 68 (3): 43–50. doi:IO.I037//0022-006X.68.3.438

Mattingly, C. (2005) 'Toward a vulnerable ethics of research practice', *Interdisciplinary Journal for Social Study of Health, Illness and Medicine*, 9, 453–71.

McGilchrist, I. (2019) *The Master and his Emissary* (2nd edn). Newhaven, CT: Yale University Press.

Mead, G.H. (1934/2015) *Mind, Self and Society: The Definitive Edition*. Chicago: University of Chicago Press.

Mead, G.H. and Morris, C.W. (1934/1967) *Mind, Self and Society: From the Standpoint of a Social Behaviourist*. Chicago: University of Chicago Press.

Mellor, K. and Schiff, E. (1975) 'Discounting', *Transactional Analysis Journal*, 5 (3): 295–302.

Merleau-Ponty, M. (1969) (A. Fisher, ed.) *The Essential Writings of Merleau-Ponty* New York: Harcourt.

Micholt, N. (1985). 'Het driehoekigkontrakt: uitbreiding en aanwending' [Three-cornered contract: Applications and expansions]. *Strook*, 7 (2): 6–21.

Micholt, N. (1992) 'Psychological distance and group interventions', *Transactional Analysis Journal*, 22 (4): 228–33.

Nietzsche, F. (1966) *Beyond Good and Evil* (translated by W. Kaufmann from original published 1886). New York: Random House.

Norcross, J.C. and Lambert, M.J. (2019) 'Evidence-based psychotherapy relationships: the third task force'. In J.C. Norcross and M.J. Lambert (eds), *Psychotherapy Relationships that Work: Evidence-based Therapist Contributions* (3rd edn). Oxford: Oxford University Press, pp. 1–23.

O'Fallon, T. (2012) 'Development and consciousness: growing up is waking up', *Spanda Journal*, 3: 97–103.

Ogden, P. and Minton, K. (2000) 'Sensorimotor psychotherapy: one method for processing traumatic memory', *Traumatology*, 6 (3): 149–73. doi.org/10.1177/153476560000600302

Ogden, P., Minton, K. and Pain, C. (2006) *Trauma and the Body: A Sensorimotor Approach to Psychotherapy.* New York: W.W. Norton & Company.

Orlinsky, D.E., Grawe, K. and Parks, B.K. (1994) 'Process and outcome in psychotherapy' In A.E. Bergin and S.L. Garfield (eds), *Handbook of Psychotherapy and Behavior Change* (4th edn). New York: Wiley.

Parlett, M. (1991) 'Reflections on field theory', *British Gestalt Journal,* 1 (1).

Perls, F. (1969/1992) *Gestalt Therapy Verbatim.* Highland, NY: The Gestalt Journal Press.

Perls, F., Hefferline, R. and Goodman, P. (1951) *Gestalt Therapy: Excitement and Growth in the Human Personality.* Gouldsboro, ME: The Gestalt Journal Press.

Phillips, A. (1998) *The Beast in the Nursery.* London: Faber & Faber.

Polster, E. (1987) *Every Person's Life is Worth a Novel.* Gouldsboro, ME: The Gestalt Journal Press.

Pope, K.S. and Vasquez, M.J.T. (2007) *Ethics in Psychotherapy and Counselling: A Practical Guide* (3rd edn). San Francisico, CA: Jossey-Bass.

Porges, S.W. (2009) 'The polyvagal theory: new insights into adaptive reactions of the autonomic nervous system', *Cleveland Clinic Journal of Medicine*, 4 (2): S86–S90.

Porges, S. (2011) *The Polyvagal Theory: Neurophysiological Foundations of Emotions, Attachment, Communication and Self-regulation.* New York: Norton.

Proctor, B. (2006) 'Contracting in supervision'. In C. Sills (ed.) *Contracts in Counselling and Psychotherapy.* London: Sage, pp. 161–74.

Rogers, C. (1951) *Client-Centered Therapy.* London: Constable.

Safran, J. D., Muran, J. C., Samstag, L. W. and Stevens, C. (2002), 'Repairing therapeutic alliance ruptures'. In: *A Guide to Psychotherapy Relationships That Work: Effective Elements of the Therapy Relationship,* In J. C. Norcross (ed.). New York: Oxford Universities Press, pp. 235–254.

Safran, J. D. (2003). 'The relational turn, the therapeutic alliance, and psychotherapy research: Strange bedfellows or postmodern marriage?', *Contemporary Psychoanalysis*, 39 (3): 449–475.

Safran, J.D. and Muran, J.C. (2006) 'Has the concept of the therapeutic alliance outlived its usefulness?' *Psychotherapy: Theory, Research, Practice, Training*, 43 (3): 286–91.

Safran, J.D. and Kraus, J. (2014) 'Alliance ruptures, impasses, and enactments: a relational perspective', *American Psychological Association*, 51 (3): 381–7.

Safran, J.D., Muran, J.C. and Eubanks-Carter, C. (2011) 'Repairing alliance ruptures', *Psychotherapy,* 48, 80–7. doi:10.1037/a0022140

Safran, J.D., Muran, J.C., Samstag, L.W. and Stevens, C. (2002) 'Repairing therapeutic alliance ruptures'. In J.C. Norcross (ed.) *A Guide to Psychotherapy Relationships that Work: Effective Elements of the Therapy Relationship*. New York: Oxford University Press, pp. 235–54.

Schore, A.N. (2003) *Affect Regulation and the Repair of the Self*. Norton.

Schore, A.N. (2009) 'Right brain affect regulation: an essential mechanism of development, trauma dissociation and psychotherapy'. In D. Fosha, D.J Siegel and M.F. Soloman (eds), *The Healing Power of Emotion*. New York: W.W. Norton.

Schore, A. (2016) *Affect Regulation and the Origin of the Self, The Neurobiology of Emotional Development*. Routledge.

Schore, A.W. (2019) *Right Brain Psychotherapy*. New York: W.W. Norton.

Schore, J.R., Schore, A. N. (2008) 'Modern attachment theory: The central role of affect-regulation in development and treatment', *Clinical Social Work Journal*, 36, 9–20.

Siegel, D. (1999) *The Developing Mind: How Relationships and the Brain Interact to Shape Who We Are*. New York: The Guilford Press.

Siegel, D. (2010) *Mindsight: Transform Your Brain with the New Science of Kindness*. Oneworld.

Siegel, D. (2018). *Aware: The Science and Practice of Presence - The Groundbreaking Meditation Practice*. New York, NY: Penguin Publishing Group.

Sills, C. (2006) *Contracts in Counselling and Psychotherapy*. London: Sage.

Sills, C. (2012) 'The coaching contract: a mutual commitment'. In E. de Haan and C. Sills (eds), *Coaching Relationships*. London: Sage, pp. 93–110.

Sills, C. and Salters, D. (1991) 'The comparative script system'. *ITA News*, 31 (11): 15.

Sills, C., Lapworth, P. and Desmond, B. (2012) *An Introduction to Gestalt*. London: Sage.

Silsbee, D. (2008) *Presence-based Coaching: Cultivating Self-generative Leaders through Mind, Body and Heart*. Hoboken, NJ: Jossey-Bass.

Skinner, D. (2012) 'Outside forces in the coaching room'. In E. de Haan and C. Sills (eds), *Coaching Relationships*. London: Sage, pp. 111–24.

Spinelli, E. (2005) *The Interpreted World: An Introduction to Phenomenological Psychology* (2nd edn). London: Sage.

Spinelli, E. (2010) 'Existential coaching'. In E. Cox, T. Bachkirova and D. Clutterbuck (eds), *The Complete Handbook of Coaching*. London: Sage.

Stacey, R. (2001) *Complex Responsive Processes in Organizations*. London: Routledge.

Stacey, R. (2003) *Strategic Management and Organisational Dynamics: The Challenge of Complexity* (4th edn). Harlow: Financial Times/Prentice Hall.

Stacey, R., Griffin, D. and Shaw, P. (2000) *Complexity and Management: Fad or Radical Challenge to Systems Thinking?* London: Routledge.

Stark, M. (2024) 'Five modes of therapeutic action'. Webinar, 22 March.

Stern, D. (1985) *The Interpersonal World of the Infant: A View from Psychoanalysis and Developmental Psychology*. New York: Basic Books.

Stolorow. R.D. (2013) 'Intersubjective-systems theory: a phenomenological–contextualist psychoanalytic perspective', *Psychoanalytic Dialogues*, 23 (4): 383–9.

Stolorow, R. and Atwood, G. (1992) *Contexts of Being: The Intersubjective Foundations of Psychological life*. Hillsdale, NJ: The Analytic Press.

Stuthridge, J. (2015) 'All the world's a stage: games, enactment and countertransference', *Transactional Analysis Journal*, 45 (2): 104–16.

Stuthridge, J. and Sills, C. (2019) 'Psychological games in the consulting room', *International Journal of Psychotherapy*, 23 (3).

Torbert, B. (2004) *Action Inquiry: The Secret of Timely and Transforming Leadership*. Oakland, CA: Berrett Koehler.

Tudor, K. (2006) 'Contracts, Complexity and Change' in C. Sills (ed.) *Contracts in Counselling and Psychotherapy*. London: Sage pp. 119–136.

Tudor, K. (2008) '"Take it": a sixth driver', *Transactional Analysis Journal*, 38 (1): 43–57.

Tudor, K. (2025, in press) *Keynote speeches on mental health and psychotherapy: Psyche and Society*. London: Routledge.

Urbinati, N. (2015) *The Tyranny of the Moderns*. Newhaven, CT: Yale University Press.

Vasisht, R. (2021) 'Self fulfilling prophecies', Linkedin, 12 November (accessed 24 April 2024).

Wachtel, P.L. (2008) *Relational Theory and the Practice of Psychotherapy*. New York: Guilford Press.

Wainwright, R. (2016) Personal communication.

Wampold, B.E. (2001) *The Great Psychotherapy Debate: Model, Methods and Findings*. Mahwah, NJ: Lawrence Erlbaum Associates.

Western, S. (2012) *Coaching and Mentoring: A Critical Text*. London: Sage.

Western, S. (2013) *Leadership: A Critical Text* (2nd edn). London: Sage.

Wheeler, G. (2000) *Beyond Individualism: Toward a New Understanding of Self, Relationship and Experience*. Cambridge, MA: GIC Press.

Winnicott, D.W. (1965) *The Family and Individual Development*. London: Tavistock.

Winnicott, D.W. (1971) *Playing and Reality*. London: Tavistock.

Worden, W. (2018) *Grief Counselling and Grief Therapy* (5th edn). New York: Routledge.

Yontef, G. (2007) 'The power of the immediate moment in Gestalt therapy', *Journal of Contemporary Psychotherapy*, 37 (1): 17–23.

Zinker, J.C. (1977) *Creative Process in Gestalt Therapy*. London: Brunner/Mazel.

INDEX

Page numbers in *italics* refer to figures.

Zeitfracht Medien GmbH
Ferdinand-Jühlke-Straße 7
99095 Erfurt, Deutschland
produktsicherheit@kolibri360.de